BOOKS BY ALBERT E. KAHN

Sabotage!*
The Plot Against the Peace*
The Great Conspiracy*
High Treason
The Game of Death
Notes on a National Scandal
Days with Ulanova
Smetana and the Beetles
The Unholy Hymnal
*With Michael Sayers

Joys & Sorrows

Pablo Casals

His own story as told to Albert E. Kahn.

EEL
PIE
PUBLISHING

First published in paperback in 1981 by
Eel Pie Publishing Ltd., 45 Broadwick Street, London W1V 1FS.

First published in the United Kingdom in 1970 by
Macdonald and Co., and in the United States by Simon and Schuster.

Copyright ©1970 by Albert E. Kahn.

ISBN 0 906008 30 1

Printed and bound in Great Britain by
R. J. Acford, Industrial Estate, Chichester, Sussex.

CONTENTS

LIST OF ILLUSTRATIONS

PREFATORY NOTE
by Albert E. Kahn

When I first discussed with Pablo Casals the possibility of my writing a book on him, I had in mind a work quite different from the present one. The book I then envisioned was one depicting—in words and photographs—his daily life and work, and presenting an intimate contemporaneous portrait of him as an artist and as a man. Both the text and photographs were to be by me.

During my preparatory work on the book, I traveled extensively with Casals in this country and abroad, attending his concerts, master classes, performances of his oratorio El Pessebre, and music festivals in which he participated. Periodically I visited him at his home in Puerto Rico. Besides photographing his diverse and indefatigable activities, I kept detailed notes or made tape recordings of our conversations, which sometimes consisted of informal chats and sometimes of structured question-and-answer exchanges regarding his past experiences and his views on a wide range of subjects. To supplement my knowledge of his earlier years, I made a survey of his papers and memorabilia at his residence at Molitg-les-Bains, France, and his former home at San Salvador, Spain.

The more I learned about Casals, the more dissatisfied I became with my original concept of the book. His career spanned such a momentous panorama of history, and the drama of his life held such rich and human import, that I grew steadily more aware of the limitations of a book which concentrated on the present and failed to merge it fully with the past. There was, moreover, such color and cadence to Casals' own words, so natural a poetry in his personal reminiscences and reflections, that his voice seemed irrevocably wedded to the telling of his story.

For a time I experimented with the approach of devoting the textual portion of the book to my questions and his answers from our conversations, but the results were frustrating. The form had a mechanical quality, and my questions seemed not only superfluous but a distracting intrusion. It became increasingly clear to me that Casals' words should stand alone.

The idea then occurred to me of eliminating my questions altogether and coordinating Casals' recollections and comments into a unity of narrative, mood and subject matter. I discussed this approach with Casals, and he agreed to it. Gradually the book assumed its present form.

There is one matter to be clarified. Over the years Casals has consistently declined to write an autobiography. As he himself put it, characteristically, in one of his letters to me, "I do not happen to feel my life deserves commemoration in an autobiography. I have only done what I had to do." It should then be stated that this book is not to be regarded as Casals' autobiography. An autobiography is, of course, a man's own portrait of himself; and this book is inevitably in part my portrait of Casals. While the words in the book are Casals', its structure is of my devising; and I am responsible for the determination of much of its content. Had Casals written his own story, he might of course have chosen to emphasize different aspects of his life.

This book, then, is offered as a portrait of Casals, delineated by his memories and observations which I have set down over the past several years and woven into this form. To the extent that I have shaped this work from his own words, I have sought to portray him, above all, as a man whose life is a testament to his credo of "the indivisible affinity between art and human values."

i

Age and Youth

On my last birthday I was ninety-three years old. That is not young, of course. In fact, it is older than ninety. But age is a relative matter. If you continue to work and to absorb the beauty in the world about you, you find that age does not necessarily mean getting old. At least, not in the ordinary sense. I feel many things more intensely than ever before, and for me life grows more fascinating.

Not long ago my friend Sasha Schneider brought me a letter addressed to me by a group of musicians in the Caucasus Mountains in the Soviet Union. This was the text of the letter:

DEAR HONORABLE MAESTRO—

I have the pleasure on behalf of the Georgian Caucasian Orchestra to invite you to conduct one of our concerts. You will be the first musician of your age who receives the distinction of conducting our orchestra.

Never in the history of our orchestra have we permitted a man under one hundred years to conduct. All of the members of our orchestra are over one hundred years old. But we have heard of your talents as a conductor, and we feel that, despite your youthfulness, an exception should be made in your case.

We expect a favorable response as soon as possible.
We pay travel expenses and of course shall provide living
accommodations during your stay with us.

Respectfully,
ASTAN SHLARBA
President, 123 years old

Sasha is a man with a sense of humor; he likes to play a
joke. That letter was one of his jokes; he had written it himself. But I must admit I took it seriously at first. And why?
Because it did not seem to me implausible that there should
be an orchestra composed of musicians older than a hundred. And, indeed, I was right! That portion of the letter
was not a joke. There is such an orchestra in the Caucasus.
Sasha had read about it in the London *Sunday Times*. He
showed me the article, with photographs of the orchestra.
All of its members were more than a hundred years old.
There were about thirty of them—they rehearse regularly
and give periodic concerts. Most of them are farmers who
continue to work in the fields. The oldest of the group, Astan Shlarba, is a tobacco grower who also trains horses.
They are splendid-looking men, obviously full of vitality.
I should like to hear them play sometime—and, in fact, to
conduct them, if the opportunity arose. Of course I am not
sure they would permit this, in view of my inadequate age.

There is often something to be learned from jokes, and
it was so in this case. In spite of their age, those musicians
have not lost their zest for life. How does one explain this?
I do not think the answer lies simply in their physical con-
stitutions or in something unique about the climate in which
they live. It has to do with their attitude toward life; and I
believe that their ability to work is due in no small measure
to the fact they *do* work. Work helps prevent one from getting old. I, for one, cannot dream of retiring. Not now or

ever. Retire? The word is alien and the idea inconceivable to me. I don't believe in retirement for anyone in my type of work, not while the spirit remains. My work is my life. I cannot think of one without the other. To "retire" means to me to begin to die. The man who works and is never bored is never old. Work and interest in worthwhile things are the best remedy for age. Each day I am reborn. Each day I must begin again.

For the past eighty years I have started each day in the same manner. It is not a mechanical routine but something essential to my daily life. I go to the piano, and I play two preludes and fugues of Bach. I cannot think of doing otherwise. It is a sort of benediction on the house. But that is not its only meaning for me. It is a rediscovery of the world of which I have the joy of being a part. It fills me with awareness of the wonder of life, with a feeling of the incredible marvel of being a human being. The music is never the same for me, never. Each day it is something new, fantastic and unbelievable. That is Bach, like nature, a miracle!

I do not think a day passes in my life in which I fail to look with fresh amazement at the miracle of nature. It is there on every side. It can be simply a shadow on a mountainside, or a spider's web gleaming with dew, or sunlight on the leaves of a tree. I have always especially loved the sea. Whenever possible, I have lived by the sea, as for these past twelve years here in Puerto Rico. It has long been a custom of mine to walk along the beach each morning before I start to work. True, my walks are shorter than they used to be, but that does not lessen the wonder of the sea. How mysterious and beautiful is the sea! how infinitely variable! It is never the same, never, not from one moment to the next, always in the process of change, always becoming something different and new.

My earliest recollections are associated with the sea. You

might say I discovered the sea when I was still an infant. Then it was the Mediterranean on the coast of Catalonia near the town of Vendrell, where I was born. When I was less than a year old, my mother began taking me to the nearby seaside hamlet of San Salvador. She took me there, she later told me, for the sea air. There was a small church at San Salvador that we would visit, an old church of Romanesque design. Light sifted through the windows, and the only sound was the whisper of the sea. It seems to me that this was the beginning of my conscious life—a sense of sunlight and the sound of the sea. As I grew older, I would remain for hours gazing from those windows at the sea, marveling at how it stretched endlessly away, and how the waves marched tirelessly to the shore and the clouds formed changing patterns in the sky. It was a sight that never ceased to enthrall me.

A man who acted as a caretaker lived beside the church in a primitive dwelling with an earth floor. He was an old sea dog, a small gnarled man who walked with a limp. He had a very high voice. He loved to tell me stories about his adventures at sea. I don't think he knew how to read or write, but I learned a great deal from him. He seemed to know everything, especially about the ways of nature. His name was Pau and his wife's name was Senda, and people called him "El Pau de la Senda." We became close friends. He would take me for strolls along the beach, and it was he who taught me how to swim. Friends of ours loaned us the use of their cottage at San Salvador. There was nothing fancy about the place, but how we loved it! I went there often with my mother.

I have repeatedly tried to write about my mother. I have wanted to record her as she was. But what I have written has never been right. I have looked at the words and said, No, this will not do, I cannot write about her. I have known

Casals' mother, Pilar Defilló de Casals

many people during my life, and among them remarkable individuals, extraordinary personalities, men and women of rare abilities and talents. I have known artists and statesmen, scholars and scientists and kings. But I have never known anyone like my mother. She dominates the memory of my childhood and youth, and her presence has remained with me throughout the years. Under all sorts of circumstances, in times of difficulty and when there were important decisions to be made, I have asked myself what she would do, and I have acted accordingly. It is forty years since my mother died, but she has continued to be my guide. Even now she is with me.

My mother was born in Mayagüez, Puerto Rico. Her parents came from Catalonia and were members of distinguished Catalan families. When she was still a young woman, just eighteen, my grandmother brought her to Spain to visit relatives in Vendrell. Her father was already dead. He had been a man of strong democratic principles, who opposed the autocratic and oppressive rule of Spain in Puerto Rico. The regime persecuted and tortured liberals, and when he could no longer endure the ordeal, this good man killed himself. A brother of my mother also died by his own hand for the same reason. Those were bitter times for the Puerto Rican people.

It was in Vendrell that my mother met my father. He was then in his early twenties. He was the church organist, and he gave piano lessons. My mother became one of his pupils, and they fell in love. When they were married, my mother gave away her lovely clothes and began wearing simple inexpensive things. It was her way of saying she was now the wife of a poor man. Years later, when my father was dead, and I was already making a success with my career, I once came to her and said, "Mother, you are so beautiful, you should wear some jewelry, perhaps a small pearl brooch.

Please let me get you one." She said, "Pablo, you are making money; you will become richer. But I shall always be the wife of a poor man." And she would not wear jewelry. That was how she was.

There was no medical care to speak of in Vendrell at the time of my mother's marriage. When children were born, a woman who was the wife of the coal dealer acted as midwife. No doubt he was a good man at his trade, but his wife knew little about delivering children. Many infants died from infections and other complications. Seven of my mother's eleven children died at birth. I myself almost did not survive. I was born with the umbilical cord twisted around my neck. My face was black, and I nearly choked to death. Though my mother had a tender heart, she never spoke of her grief at the death of her children.

For my mother, the highest law was a man's own conscience. She used to say, "In principle, I do not respect the law." She would say that one law might have some merit and another none, and that a man had to decide for himself what was right and what was wrong. She knew that certain laws can serve some people and injure others, as in Spain today, where the law in general benefits the few and harms the many. This understanding came from within her. She always acted on principle, not on what others said but on what she herself knew to be right. When my brother Enrique was nineteen, he was called to serve in the Spanish army in accordance with the law of the time. He came to my mother. I was there, and the scene is stamped on my memory. "My son," she told Enrique, "you do not have to kill anybody, and nobody has to kill you. You were not born to kill or be killed. Go away . . . leave the country." So Enrique fled from Spain. He went to Argentina. My mother felt a special tenderness for Enrique, who was the youngest of her children, but she did not see him again for eleven years. He returned home when there was an amnesty for those who had broken the conscription law. I think that if all the mothers of the world would tell their sons, "You were not born to be killers or to be killed in war. Do not fight," there would be no more war.

When my mother told my brother Enrique to go away, it was not for her simply a matter of saving the life of her son. It was a matter of doing what was right. On another occasion there was an epidemic of cholera in our region. It was a frightful calamity. One moment you would see a man walking and talking naturally, and an hour later he would be dead. Thousands died in the area, and many in Vendrell. Almost all the doctors died. We were making our home then in San Salvador. My brother Luis, who was about eighteen, used to go away every evening to Vendrell. He would go to the houses where the people had died from cholera and take their bodies during the night to the cemetery. "Someone must do it," he said. The danger of contagion was very great. My mother of course knew that he was risking his life every day, but she never said a word, not a single word, to stop him from doing what he felt he had to do. There was no equivocation in my mother. She was straight, always straight. It was so in small matters as well as large.

She had no use for petty regulations. When I was a young man and giving many concerts, I had several bank accounts. One of them was in Barcelona, and I used to give the receipts for my deposits to my mother. She would put them away and keep them for me. Once the bank asked me for a receipt they had given me the previous year, and I told my mother. She looked for it but could not find it.

I said to her, "Well, mother dear, they want to see it."

"Why, Pablo?" she said.

I said, "Because it is the rule."

"The rule? Don't they know the money is yours?"

"Yes, they know it."

"Well, then, it is not necessary to give them the receipt. They know the money is yours. You tell them that."

I informed the bank that I couldn't find the receipt, and they said it would be all right, I could forget about the matter.

"What did I tell you?" my mother said. "You see it wasn't necessary to give them that receipt."

She regarded rigid formalities as foolish. She was that way in everything.

When I was still a small boy, my father told me, "Pablo, when you grow up, you will see machines that fly. Mark my words; it will surely happen." Today that does not seem remarkable; jet planes fly over my house faster than sound —though what a sound *they* make!—and children take it for granted that they themselves will soon visit the moon. But when I was born, the automobile had not yet been invented. My father had a lively imagination and an inquiring mind. Music was his great love but only one of his interests. Physics fascinated him. He was especially interested in scientific discoveries. He had been born in Barcelona and lived all his adult life in Vendrell; he could not afford to travel; but he managed to get periodicals from other countries— from France in particular—and he followed the latest developments in science. He himself had an unusual ability with his hands; it seemed to me that he could make almost anything. He had a special workroom in our house, a room which was kept locked, and he used to spend hours in it. He made all sorts of things out of wood and other materials. He was a real craftsman. Once he made me a bicycle. He even made a clock out of wood; I still have it at my house in San Salvador, though I have not seen it since I went into exile thirty years ago. He was very painstaking with his

work, a perfectionist. He was patient about everything—he
suffered badly from asthma but he never complained. He
was a quiet and gentle man; I cannot recall hearing him
raise his voice. At the same time, he was a man of strong
convictions, an ardent liberal, and during the Carlist wars
in Catalonia he had risked his life for the Republican cause.
That was shortly before he married my mother. Naturally,
he was a staunch advocate of autonomy for Catalonia.

My father's life was built around music. If he had had a
real musical education, he could have been an accomplished
composer or an outstanding pianist. But he was satisfied to
be what he was, the church organist at Vendrell, and to give
piano and singing lessons, and to write the songs and other
music he composed. He organized a small choral society in
the village—that was about a hundred years ago, and the
society still exists. He played at the village festivals and
dances, and when he did, he put his whole heart and soul
into his playing. Beauty was his aim, and he was without
pretension.

My father recognized that I had musical talent as a child,
but he was such a musician himself that he took it for
granted his son should also be one. He never said, "Oh, my
boy is a wonderful musician," or anything like that. He saw
nothing unusual in my ability to play and compose at an
early age; it seemed entirely natural to him. My mother's
attitude was very different. She didn't talk about my ability
either; but she was convinced that I had a special gift and
that everything should be done to nourish it. My father did
not believe I could earn a living as a musician; he knew
from experience how hard it was to do this. He thought it
would be more practical for me to have a trade; and, in fact,
when I was still a youngster he made plans with a carpenter
friend for me to become his apprentice. I have always regarded manual labor as creative and looked with respect—

Casals' father, Carlos Casals

and, yes, wonder—at people who work with their hands. It seems to me that their creativity is no less than that of a violinist or a painter. It is of a different sort, that is all. And if it had not been for my mother's conviction and determination that music was my destiny, it is quite conceivable that I would have become a carpenter. But I do not think I would have made a very good one. Unlike my father, I never had a knack for making things or even doing the simplest manual tasks. Only recently I couldn't open a container of cottage cheese! It exasperated me; I told my wife, my lovely Marta, "You know, I can't do anything with my hands!" She said that was not entirely true, and she pointed to my cello, which was standing in the corner. She was right, of course—there have been some compensations.

ii

Nativity

The tale of the Nativity has always had a special meaning for me.

One of the first compositions on which I worked—I was six or seven at the time—was the music my father and I wrote for a performance of *Els Pastorets*, the "Adoration of the Shepherds." The pageant took place at the Catholic Center in Vendrell, and I played the part of the devil, who plotted—devilishly, of course—all sorts of cunning schemes to prevent the shepherds and Wise Men from getting to Bethlehem.

More than seventy years later, when I was already living in exile from Spain after the Civil War, I began the custom of concluding concerts and music festivals with the melody of an old Catalan folk song which is actually a Christmas carol. It is called *El Cant del Ocells*, the "Song of the Birds." The melody then came to be known as the nostalgic theme of the Spanish refugees. Today in the village of Molitg-les-Bains in the French Pyrenees, adjoining the lovely spa of the Hotel Grand Thermal, I have a cottage at which I have stayed in recent years during the Prades music festivals. The owner of the hotel has placed a carillon of fifteen bells in a tower there. I recorded the "Song of the Birds" for the bells, and every hour you can hear its haunting melody sing out, echoing among the mountains. On the largest bell is an inscription which says that through this song I speak of the sorrow and homesickness of Catalans. It adds, "May this be for them tomorrow—a song of peace and hope."

Ten years ago, when what people call the Cold War had become intense and the fear of atomic war spread through the world, I embarked on a peace crusade of my own, with the only weapon I have at my command—my music. Again, it was to the story of the Nativity that I turned. I had written an oratorio called *El Pessebre (The Manger)*, based on a poem about the Nativity by my dear friend, the Catalan writer Joan Alavedra; and I began taking this oratorio to the capitals of many lands. Through this music I have sought to draw attention to the suffering that afflicts humanity, to the fearful danger of nuclear war, and to the happiness man can attain if all men work together as brothers and in peace: so, in this nuclear age, the ancient tale of the Nativity has a special urgency for me.

How beautiful and tender is that tale, with its reverence for life and for man, the noblest expression of life! And think of its symbolism: the symbol of the mother and the child—of birth and creation; the symbol of the shepherds, common working people, who revere the newborn child with his promise of a joyous world; the symbol of the Prince of Peace, born not in a palace but in a stable. How simple and yet how profoundly meaningful!

And how much of nature comes into this tale! In the Catalan carol, "Song of the Birds," it is the eagles and the sparrows, the nightingales and the little wrens that sing a welcome to the infant, singing of him as a flower that will delight the earth with its sweet scent. And the thrushes and linnets sing that spring has come and tree leaves are unfolding and growing green.

In *El Pessebre*, the fisherman sings:

In the river that passes
The current I see!
In waves of reflection
My fish wait for me
Whose tails are dancing
And shining and sparkling
As clearly and freshly
As silver and gold.

Yet throughout this tale of the Nativity there is an awareness of man's suffering—a premonition of what the Christ child will one day endure. And this is expressed in the song of a woman weaving a shroud for that future time of pain and torment. . . .

Finally, the angels and shepherds sing together, "Glory to God! Peace to the earth! War shall forever disappear. Peace to all men!"

I have said that when I was seven I worked on my first composition on the Nativity, but of course I knew the tale before that. One of my very earliest and most indelible memories is of a Christmas Mass at the church in Vendrell. I was then five years old and had started to sing in the choir a few months before. In Vendrell there was no midnight Mass, and I was to sing on Christmas at *la misa del gallo*—the "Mass of the Cock"—which was held at five o'clock in the morning. I hardly slept the night before, and it was pitch-black when my father came into my room to tell me it was time to get ready to go to the services. When we stepped out of the house it was dark and cold—so cold that bundled up as I was, the chill went right through my clothes and I shivered as we walked, though I did not shiver only because of the cold. It was all so mysterious; I felt that something wonderful was about to happen. High overhead the heavens were still full of stars, and as we walked

in silence I held my father's hand, feeling he was my protector and guide. The village was hushed, and in the dark
narrow streets there were moving figures, shadowy and
spectral and silent too, moving toward the church in the
starry night. Then, suddenly, there was a burst of light—
flooding from the open doors of the church. We moved into
that light and into the church, silently, with the other people. My father played the organ, and when I sang, it was
my heart that was singing and I poured out everything
that was in me. . . .

From infancy I was surrounded by music. You might
say music was for me an ocean in which I swam like a little
fish. Music was inside me and all about me; it was the air
I breathed from the time I could walk. To hear my father
play the piano was an ecstasy for me. When I was two or
three, I would sit on the floor beside him as he played, and
I would press my head against the piano in order to absorb
the sound more completely. I could sing in tune before
I could speak clearly; notes were as familiar to me as words.
My father used to have my little brother Artur and me
stand behind the piano—we were too small to see over
the top of it—and he would stand in front of the piano
with his back to it. Reaching behind him and spreading out
the fingers of both hands, he would strike chords at random
on the piano. "Now what notes did I play?" he would
say. And we would have to name all the notes in the dis-
sonant chords he had played. Then he would do it again,
and again. Artur was two years younger than I was—he
died at five from spinal meningitis. He was a lovely little
boy, and he had a sharper ear for music than mine.

I began playing the piano when I was four years old. I
must say I am glad I learned to play the piano at the very
beginning. For me it is the best of all instruments—yes,

despite my love of the cello. On a piano you can play anything that has been written. Violinists, for example, have a big repertory and many do not have or take the time to learn what composers have written for other instruments or for the orchestra as a whole; and so, in that sense, many are not complete musicians. With the piano it is a different matter; the instrument encompasses everything. That is why everyone who wants to devote his life to music should know how to play the piano, whether or not he prefers another instrument. I can say that I became a good pianist—although I am afraid that I no longer am. I have no technique now. But every morning of course I still play the piano.

It was my father who taught me to play the piano and gave me my first lessons in composition. It was he who taught me how to sing. I was five when I became a second soprano in the church choir. It was a momentous event in my life—to actually be a member of the choir and to sing while my father played the organ! I was paid for every service; my fee amounted to the sum of ten cents; and so one might say that this was my first professional job as a musician. It was for me a very serious duty, and I felt responsible not only for my own singing but for the singing of the other boys as well. I was the youngest member of the choir, but I would say, "Watch it, now! Be careful with that note." It would seem I already had aspirations to be a conductor.

Sometimes I awakened in the morning to the sound of folk songs, the villagers—fishermen and men who worked in the vineyards—singing as they went to work. Sometimes in the evening there were dances in the plaza and sometimes festivals at which the *gralla* was played. The *gralla* is a reed instrument which, I think, is probably of Moorish origin—it resembles an oboe and has a very strident sound.

Every day I would hear my father playing the piano or the organ. There were his songs and church music and compositions of the masters. He took me to all the services at the church—the Gregorian chant, the chorals and the organ voluntaries became part of my daily life. And then, too, there were always the wonderful sounds of nature, the sound of the sea, the sound of the wind moving through the trees, the delicate singing of the birds, the infinitely varied melody of the human voice, not only in song but in speech. What a wealth of music! It sustained and nourished me.

I was curious about all instruments, and I wanted to play them all. By the time I was seven I was playing the violin, and I played a solo at a concert in Vendrell at the age of eight. I longed especially to play the organ. But my father said I could not touch the instrument until my feet could reach the pedals. How I waited for that day! I was never very tall, so the day took somewhat longer to arrive than it would have for another child. In fact, it seemed to me an interminable time. I kept on trying, sitting at the stool alone in the church and stretching out my feet, but—alas! —that did not help me grow any more quickly. The great moment finally came when I was nine. I hurried to my father and told him, "Father, I can touch the pedals!" He said, "Let me see." I reached out my feet and they touched —barely, but they touched. My father said, "All right, now you can play the organ." It was a lovely old instrument, made at the same time as the one that Bach used in Leipzig. It is still in the church in Vendrell.

Before long I had learned to play the organ well enough so that I sometimes took my father's place when he was ill or busy with some other work. Once when I had finished playing and was leaving the church, a friend of my father's who was a shoemaker came up to me and said, "How magnificently your father played today!" At that time, shoe-makers in our village worked in the streets, sitting on stools. This man had been sitting outside the church and listening while he worked. I told the shoemaker that my father was not well, and that I was the one who had been playing. At first he would not believe me, but I assured him it was so. He summoned his wife and told her with great excite-ment, "That was not Carlos at the organ. You will not believe me, but it was Pablito!" The shoemaker and his wife put their arms around me and kissed me; then they took me into their house and gave me biscuits and wine.

In those days, bands of itinerant musicians wandered from village to village, eking out a meager existence on whatever money the villagers could spare them. They played in the streets and at village dances. They often dressed in bizarre costumes, and performed on a weird vari-ety of instruments, often of their own contriving. I always greeted their arrival with great excitement. One day a group of three such musicians came to Vendrell; they called them-selves Los Tres Bemoles, or The Three Flats. I made my way to the front of the crowd that had gathered in the plaza to hear them, and I crouched there on the cobble-stones completely enthralled, enchanted by the appearance of the players—they were dressed as clowns—and I listened spellbound to every note they played. I was especially fasci-nated by their instruments. They had mandolins, bells, gui-tars, and even instruments made out of kitchen utensils like teapots, cups and glasses—I think these instruments must surely have been the forerunners of some of the curious contraptions that are played in jazz orchestras to-day. One man played on a broom handle that was strung something like a cello—though I had never seen or even heard of a cello at that time. For some reason—possibly I had some sort of prescience!—that broom-handle instrument fascinated me most of all. I couldn't take my eyes off it. It sounded wonderful to me. When I went home, I told my father breathlessly about it. He laughed, but I talked so passionately about it that he said, "All right, Pablo, I'll make you an instrument like it." And he did—though I must say it was a considerable improvement on the broom handle and sounded much better. He fashioned it out of a gourd, with a single string. I suppose you might say that this instrument was my first cello. I still have it at San Salvador. I have kept it in a glass case, like a real museum treasure.

On that homemade contrivance I learned to play many of the songs my father wrote, as well as popular melodies that reached our village from the outer world. Years later, when I was visiting the nearby ancient monastery of Santes Creus, I met an old innkeeper who said that he remembered hearing me play that strange instrument one night, when I was a boy of nine, in the cloisters of the monastery. And I too remembered that night—when I played in the moon-light and the music echoed among the shadows and against the crumbling white monastery walls. . . .

I see no particular merit in the fact that I was an artist at the age of eleven. I was born with an ability, with music in me, that is all. No special credit was due me. The only credit we can claim is for the use we make of the talent we are given. That is why I urge young musicians: "Don't be vain because you happen to have talent. You are not responsible for that; it was not of your doing. What you do with your talent is what matters. You must cherish this gift. Do not demean or waste what you have been given. Work—work constantly and nourish it."

Of course the gift to be cherished most of all is that of life itself. One's work should be a salute to life.

iii

The Opening World

When I was eleven years old, I heard the cello played for the first time. That was the beginning of a long and cherished companionship! A trio had come to play at a concert in Vendrell—a pianist, a violinist and a cellist. My father took me to the concert. It was held at the small hall of the Catholic Center, with an audience of townspeople, fishermen and peasants, who, as always for such an occasion, were dressed in their Sunday clothes. The cellist was Josep García, a teacher at the Municipal School of Music in Barcelona; he was a handsome man with a high forehead and a handlebar mustache; and his figure somehow seemed fitted to his instrument. When I saw his cello I was fascinated by it—I had never seen one before. From the moment I heard the first notes I was overwhelmed. I felt as if I could not breathe. There was something so tender, beautiful and human—yes, so very human—about the sound. I had never heard such a beautiful sound before. A radiance filled me. When the first composition was ended, I told my father, "Father, that is the most wonderful instrument I have ever heard. That is what I want to play."

After the concert I kept talking to my father about the cello, pleading with him to get me one. From that time, more than eighty years ago, I was wedded to the instrument.

It would be my companion and friend for the rest of my life. I had of course found joy in the violin, the piano and other instruments, but for me the cello was something special and unique. I began playing my violin holding it like a cello.

My mother understood what had happened. She told my father, "Pablo shows such enthusiasm for the cello that he must have the chance really to study it. There is no teacher here in Vendrell who is qualified to teach him properly. We must arrange for him to go to the School of Music in Barcelona."

My father was astonished. "What in the world are you talking about?" he asked. "How can Pablo possibly go to Barcelona? We simply do not have the money."

My mother said, "We will find a way. I will take him there. Pablo is a musician. This is his nature. This is what he was made to be. He must go anywhere necessary. There is no other choice."

My father was not at all convinced—he was, in fact, already thinking about my following the trade of a carpenter in order to earn a living. "You have delusions of grandeur," he told my mother.

Their discussions on the subject became more and more frequent and intense. It troubled me greatly. I felt I was to blame for the disagreement between them. I asked myself how I could end it, but I didn't know what to do. Finally, my father reluctantly gave in. He wrote a letter to the Municipal School of Music in Barcelona asking if they would accept me as a pupil. He also said that I would need a small cello, three-quarter size, and asked if they knew an instrument maker who could make one for me.

Even so, after the school had responded favorably and as the time approached for my going to Barcelona, my father continued to express misgivings.

"Dear Carlos," my mother would tell him, "you may be

sure that this is right. This is what has to be. It is the only thing for Pablo."

My father would shake his head. "I do not understand, I do not understand."

And she would say, "I know that, but you must have faith. You must be confident; you must."

It was a truly remarkable thing. My mother had had some musical training, but she was not of course a musician in the sense my father was. Yet she knew what my future was to be. She had known, I believe, from the beginning; it was as if she had some special sensitivity, a peculiar pre-science. She knew; and she always acted on the knowledge with a firmness and certainty and calmness that has never ceased to amaze me. This was so not only about my study-ing in Barcelona, but in later years, on other occasions when I was at a crossroads in my career. It was so also with my younger brothers, Luis and Enrique; when they were still children, she knew the paths that they would follow. And later when I was playing concerts in many parts of the world and some success had come to me, she was happy but I would not say impressed. She had assumed this would be so.

During my life I myself have come to understand what she believed. I have come to the feeling that what happens must happen. I do not mean of course that there is nothing we can do about what we are or what we shall become. Ev-erything about us is in a constant state of change—that is the way of nature; and we ourselves are changing all the time, for we are part of nature. We have the duty always to work to change ourselves for the better. But I do believe we have our destinies.

I departed from Vendrell with mixed feelings. It was my home, the scene of my childhood. The winding streets along which I rode my bicycle, our little house with its living room where my father practiced the piano and gave lessons, the church where I spent so many hours of joy, my school chums with whom I wrestled and played games— all those dear, familiar things, I did not want to leave them. I was, after all, eleven and a half; and, even for a musician, that is not very old. Barcelona is only fifty miles or so from Vendrell; but for me it was like voyaging to another land. What would it be like? Where would I stay? Who would my friends and teachers be? At the same time, of course, I was tingling with excitement. . . . My mother traveled with me on the train. When my father tenderly embraced me at the station saying goodbye, I tried to remember what he had told me once when I had been bitten by a dog and taken to the hospital: "Say to yourself that men don't cry."

So it was that eighty years ago I went to Barcelona. Then, as now, it was a great and sprawling city with busy streets and colorful cafés, parks and museums, crowded shops and bustling wharves, where ships from many lands anchored. It was for me, in more senses than one, the gateway to the world: this city where I was destined to pass so rich a portion of my life, with whose splendid citizens I would share so many hours of happiness and creativity, with whose artists and workingmen I would form such cherished ties, this city where I would learn so much about the nobility of man —and alas, so much about man's suffering too! Half a century later, I would see this dear city under siege by the fascists, with bombing planes overhead, and militiamen and sandbags in the streets. What child could dream such things would come to pass?

My mother entered me in the Municipal School of Music in Barcelona and returned to Vendrell—she was to come back to Barcelona after a month or so and remain there with me. She had made arrangements for me to stay with some distant relatives of hers, a carpenter and his wife who lived

in a working-class neighborhood in one of the older districts of the city. They were kind and gentle people; they
treated me as if I were their own child. The carpenter—his
name was Benet— was a fantastic person. Not a large man
but absolutely fearless, he was a crusader who waged his
own one-man war against crime. I found out about it one
day when he opened a drawer and I saw to my astonishment
that it was full of knives and pistols. I asked in wonder what
all those weapons were for. He then told me of his unique
avocation. Almost every evening, after he had finished work
and eaten his supper, Benet would disappear from the
house. He would sally forth into the roughest districts of
the city—there was a good deal of crime in Barcelona in
those days. All he carried with him was a heavy ash stick,
but in his hands it was a formidable weapon. Holding that
stick—not too ostentatiously but in clear sight—he would
confront notorious criminals: robbers, thieves and other
desperadoes. He would walk up to one and tell him that he
was a bad man and had done this or that. "You must change
your ways," he would say. "Now give me your pistol." Or
knife, whichever the case might be. The criminals knew his
reputation; they had respect for him, and usually they
obeyed him. Some, of course, did not want to; and then he
used his stick. One night he came home with a knife wound.
He shrugged. "Never mind, it's nothing," he told his wife
and me. "I'll settle the affair tomorrow." The following
night he came in smiling cheerfully. "I squared things up
with that fellow," he said. He was, I suppose one might say,
an apostle of a sort. He made a very great impression upon
me.

Shortly after my arrival in Barcelona, I went to pick up
the small cello that my father had arranged to have made
for me. The instrument maker was a very affable man in
his early thirties whose name was Maire. When he gave

me the cello, he also gave me a bow. I had never held a cello before, but I immediately played something on it. Maire was astonished and delighted. . . .

I worked very hard at the music school, studying harmony and counterpoint, composition, as well as the cello and piano. My cello teacher was the same Josep García whose playing in Vendrell had had such a profound effect upon me. He belonged to the famous García family. He was related to the celebrated Manuel García, singer, composer, actor and teacher, who founded what was perhaps the most extraordinary family of singers there has ever been—his daughter was the great Maria Malibran, and his son Manuel, himself a teacher, invented the laryngoscope. Josep García was a fine cellist—I have never seen a more beautiful hand on the strings—and he was an excellent teacher. He was demanding in his discipline, and in spite of being really a gentle man, he sometimes frightened his pupils. He rarely gave signs of approval during our lessons. But sometimes when I was playing, he would turn his back to me, and he would stay like that for a long time. When he turned toward me again, he had a very strange expression on his face. I did not understand it at the time, but later I realized that he was moved. Many years afterwards, when I was in full career, I saw García in Buenos Aires, where he had gone to live. What a joyous reunion that was! He was so proud that he had been my teacher, and I was so grateful for all that he had taught me and for his tenderness with me. When we embraced, we wept.

While I was at the school in Barcelona, I began making certain changes in the then accepted technique of playing the cello. It is true I was only twelve or so at the time, but certain things are obvious even to children. And it was clear to me that there was something very awkward and unnatural in playing with a stiff arm and with one's elbows close to one's sides, as cellists were taught in those days—as a matter of fact, we had to hold a book under the armpit of our bowing arm while we were learning! That all seemed foolish to me. So at home, while I was practicing, I began to devise a method of playing which would free the arms and get rid of that very cramped and artificial position. I also felt that the technique of fingering and the action of the left hand could be improved—the hand in those days was cramped and cellists had to move it constantly up and down in fingering. I tried opening up the hand, enlarging and extending its reach, and I found I could play four notes without moving it, whereas players up until then had been able to play only three. When I began employing some of my innovations at the school, there was consternation among the students; my teacher too was rather startled at first, but he was an understanding man, as I have said, and he came to see there was a method in my seeming madness. Anyway, today nobody learns the cello with a book under his armpit!

After about six months at the school, I had made sufficient progress on the cello to enable me to secure a job playing in a café in a suburb of the city. It was a nice family place called Café Tost after its proprietor, Señor Tost. I played there every day, and my salary was four pesetas a day. We were a trio—a violin, a piano, and a cello. Our repertoire consisted mainly of light music: popular tunes of the day, familiar operatic selections, and waltzes. However, at that time my young brain was already humming with the music of the masters—of Bach, Brahms, Mendelssohn, Beethoven. Before long—and with a certain subtlety, I think, for one of my youth—I managed to begin introducing better music into the program. The customers liked it. So then I felt ready to suggest to the management and to the other members of the trio that we devote one night

a week to a program of classical music. That night proved
to be a real success. Soon I was also playing solos. Talk
spread about the music at the Café Tost and about the playing of *el nen* "the little one"—as I had come to be known.
Customers began coming from quite a distance to spend an
evening at the café. Señor Tost was pleased at this development, and he was proud of me. Sometimes he would take
me to concerts; once we heard Richard Strauss conducting
some of his works at the Teatro Lírico—Strauss was then a
young man, at the beginning of his career. The experience
had a great impact on me.

One thing about me annoyed Señor Tost—that was
when I did not arrive punctually at his café; I was supposed
to be there on the dot of nine o'clock. However, there were
exciting things to see in the city, and lots of new ideas for
a young boy to think about. I might be strolling down the
boulevard of Las Ramblas with its fascinating bird markets
and flower stalls, or exploring some neighborhood I'd never
seen before, or reading a new book, or just daydreaming in
the gardens of the Teatro Lírico; so sometimes I was late
to work. One evening Señor Tost was standing sternly in
the doorway when I arrived. He reached into his pocket and
handed me a watch. "All right," he said. "Perhaps this will
help teach you the meaning of time." It was my first watch.
I think I can say that as the years have passed I have learned
more about the meaning of time and I use time carefully
and am well organized, though sometimes Marta has to
remind me—especially when I am practicing or studying a
score—that the moment has arrived for an appointment.
For me organization is essential to creative work, and I
often repeat to my pupils this motto: "Freedom—and order!"

In the summer months, when school was out, I joined
traveling bands of musicians. We journeyed across the

La Opinion. Tarragona 2 Ágosto 1889.

En la ejecucion individual ha sobresa-
lido el niño Paulito Casals en la parte que le
ha correspondido de violoncello que la ha de-
se npeñado con el acierto de un maestro en tan
dificil arte, por lo que no dudamos en asegu-
rarle un brillante porvenir en el estudio de la
música si prosigue con la aficion de hoy y su
nnato talento musical.

ILUSTRACION MUSICAL

Barcelona,

El alumno de violoncello, D. Pablo Casals,
distinguido discipulo del Sr. García, demostró
excepcionales cualidades en la ejecución del
Allegro appassionato de nuestro malogrado Tusquets, que le valieron una ovación tan entu-
siasta como merecida. El Sr. Casals, que es un
niño todavía por su edad, ha probado en la
Escuela municipal de Música, desde el primer
año de solfeo, concurriendo ya hoy día á los
cursos superiores de violoncello, piano y com-
posición, siendo uno de los alumnos que más
la honran por su aplicación é indisputable talento.

The two earliest reviews of performances by Casals—at the respective
ages of twelve and thirteen—from a scrapbook of clippings kept by
his mother. The first review, dated August 25, 1889, reads: "In his
own performance the boy Paulito Casals was outstanding in the
violoncello part which he developed with such masterly confidence
that we have no hesitation in assuring him a brilliant future in the
study of music if he continues with his present devotion and innate
musical talent." The second review, dated December 1890, reads:
"The violoncello pupil, Don Pablo Casals, distinguished disciple of
Señor García, demonstrated exceptional qualities in the performance
of the *Allegro appassionato* of our lamented Tusquets, which brought
him an ovation as enthusiastic as it was deserved. Señor Casals, who
is still a child in years, has proven at the Municipal School of Music,
from the first year of solfeggio to his present participation in higher
courses of violoncello, piano and composition, to be one of the pupils
who has honored the school through his dedication and indisputable
talent."

Catalan countryside—in horse-drawn buses along hot and
dusty roads—from village to village, playing at fairs,
dances and festivals. We played folk music and dances—
waltzes, mazurkas, sardanas, pieces from America, everything. Often we started playing in the early evening and
continued into the morning hours. The peasants and fishermen were sturdy folk, and they could dance all night—and
all the next day, for that matter! Those summer tours were
strenuous and allowed little time for rest, but how I relished
them! And I found a special happiness in the wonderful
camaraderie with the villagers for whom I played, in the
communication between them and me when they danced,
and the look on their faces afterwards as they shouted and
applauded. We conversed through the language of music,
and in my performances ever since—whether at small recitals or before large audiences in great concert halls—I
have never lost the feeling I then came to have of intimate
understanding between myself and those for whom I
played. . . .

After a couple of years of playing at the Café Tost, I was
offered a better job. It was at the Café Pajarera. In Spanish,
pajarera means "birdcage," and the café was a large circular
building with glass walls, quite impressive-looking. There
I was paid more money, and I played in an ensemble of
seven instead of three.

I gave my first real concert in Barcelona when I was
fourteen. It was a benefit performance at the Teatro de
Novedades for a famous old actress. Her name was Con-
cepción Palá. My father, who had come to Barcelona for
the occasion, took me on the tramway. I was terribly nervous. When we got to the concert hall, I said, "Father, I've
forgotten the beginning of the piece! I can't remember a
note of it! What shall I do?" He calmed me down. That was
eighty years ago, but I've never conquered that dreadful

PRIMERA PARTE

1.º Liszt, *Rhapsodie* . . . . Sr. Bonin

2.ª Vieniausky, *Polonaise.* . . . Srtos. Bonin hermanos

3.º Beethoven, *Sonata en do menor.* . Srta. Via

4.º { Beriot, *Andante.* . . . . . . } Srtos. Bonin hermanos
{ Dancla, *Bolero.* . . . . . . }

5.º Scarlatti, *Capricho* . . . . . Srta. Via

SEGUNDA PARTE

1.º Chopin, *Polonaise.* . . . . . Sr. Bonin

2.º Opper, *Gavotte.* . . . . . . Sr. Casals

3.º Thomé, *La Sirene.* . . . . . Srta. Via

4.º Dunkler, *Polonaise.* . . . . . Sr. Casals

5.º Thalberg, *Estudio.* . . . . . Srta. Via

6.º Liszt, *Rhapsodie.* . . . . . . Srta. Via

Barcelona, 30 de Marzo 1892

Pelayo, 9, entr.º

Henrich y Comp., Suc. Ramírez

One of the first concert programs listing a performance by Casals, Barcelona, 1892

feeling of nervousness before a performance. It is always an ordeal. Before I go onstage, I have a pain in my chest. I'm tormented. The thought of a public performance is still a nightmare. . . .

My father used to come once a week from Vendrell to visit me. We would go for walks together, sometimes wandering into music shops looking for music scores; and after a few hours he would have to go back home. The repertoire of the ensemble at the Café Pajarera was broader than the Café Tost; I continued my solos, and of course I needed more music. One day I told my father I needed especially to find some new solo music for the Café Pajarera. Together we set off on the search. For two reasons I shall never forget that afternoon. First, my father bought me my first full-sized cello—how proud I was to have that wonderful instrument! Then we stopped at an old music shop near the harbor. I began browsing through a bundle of musical scores. Suddenly I came upon a sheaf of pages, crumbled and discolored with age. They were unaccompanied suites by Johann Sebastian Bach—for the cello only! I looked at them with wonder: *Six Suites for Violoncello Solo*. What magic and mystery, I thought, were hidden in those words? I had never heard of the existence of the suites; nobody—not even my teachers—had ever mentioned them to me. I forgot our reason for being at the shop. All I could do was stare at the pages and caress them. That scene has never grown dim. Even today, when I look at the cover of that music, I am back again in the old musty shop with its faint smell of the sea. I hurried home, clutching the suites as if they were the crown jewels, and once in my room I pored over them. I read and reread them. I was thirteen at the time, but for the following eighty years the wonder of my discovery has continued to grow on me. Those suites opened up a whole new world. I began playing them with indescribable excitement.

They became my most cherished music. I studied and worked at them every day for the next twelve years. Yes, twelve years would elapse and I would be twenty-five before I had the courage to play one of the suites in public at a concert. Up until then, no violinist or cellist had ever played one of the Bach suites in its entirety. They would play just a single section—a Saraband, a Gavotte or a Minuet. But I played them as a whole: from the Prelude through the five dance movements, with all the repeats that give the wonderful entity and pacing and structure of every movement, the full architecture and artistry. They had been considered academic works, mechanical, without warmth. Imagine that! How could anyone think of them as being cold, when a whole radiance of space and poetry pours forth from them! They are the very essence of Bach, and Bach is the essence of music.

It was shortly before my discovery of the Bach suites that another event occurred which was to have a far-reaching effect upon my life as an artist. I was still at the Café Tost when it happened. An important visitor came one evening to the café. He was the celebrated Catalan composer and pianist, Isaac Albéniz. With him were his friends, the violinist Enrique Arbós and the cellist Agustín Rubio. Albéniz had heard about *el nen*, the boy who was said to play so well on the cello, and he wanted to see for himself. He sat there listening intently—a small plump man of about thirty with a little beard and a mustache, smoking a long cigar. When the program was over, he came up and embraced me. I had, he said, a rare talent. "You must come with me to London!" he said—he had a buoyant, infectious air. "You must come and work with me there." I was naturally very flattered at such a proposal from this famous musician. But when he repeated it to my mother, her reception was quite different. She said she appreciated the offer but was absolutely opposed to my going. "My child is still a child," she told Albéniz. "He is much too young to go to London and to start traveling around. He must stay here in Barcelona and complete his studies. There will be plenty of time later for other things."

Albéniz could see that my mother was not a woman whose mind could be changed. He said, "All right, but your son has a great gift, and I feel I must do whatever I can to help him. Let me give you a letter of introduction to the Count de Morphy in Madrid. He is a wonderful man, a patron of the arts, a splendid musician and brilliant scholar, he is the personal adviser to Queen María Cristina. He has much influence. He can help Pablo's career. When you are ready, take the letter to him." My mother said all right, and Albéniz gave her the letter.

Three years would pass before my mother used that letter. She kept it, waiting for the time she thought appropriate; when she did use it, the moment would prove to be one of the most important milestones in my career. And it came about in so simple a way. Life is sometimes like that.

Later, Albéniz would become one of my dear friends. He was not only a great artist, a magnificent pianist, but a most amazing man.

He had been a child prodigy—he made his debut as a pianist at the Teatro Romea in Barcelona when he was four years old. When he was seven, he composed a march that came to be widely played by military bands. As a youngster, he became involved in all sorts of wild adventures. He ran away from home at thirteen and wandered all over Europe, playing the piano and getting involved in mad escapades; then he got on a ship—he was a stowaway, I think—and went to America, where he had adventures with Indians, and things of that sort. What stories he used to tell! He came back to Spain when he was still a young man. Finally he settled down in London. He had an astonishing virtuosity; he never practiced—not even for concerts; his hands were little but amazingly strong and supple. The music he composed was greatly affected by his homeland of Catalonia, by its wonderful scenery and its folk melodies, and by the Arabic derivations of some of them, too. "I am a Moor," he used to say. He had a rare sense of humor; and he was a real Bohemian. I have heard that he sold his well-known composition, *Pavana*, for the lordly sum of fifteen pesetas— the price of a ticket to a bullfight that he wanted very much to see.

The way in which Count de Morphy had first met Albéniz was typical of this artist's life. The count was traveling by train—to Switzerland, I believe—when he heard a peculiar sound under his seat. He leaned down and there, beneath his seat, he found a boy hiding. It was Albéniz, and he was hiding there of course to avoid paying the fare. "And who are you, may I inquire?" said the count. Albéniz —he was then about thirteen—replied, "I am a great artist." That was the beginning of their acquaintanceship.

Throughout my adult life I have believed in the perfectibility of man. What a marvel he is—what fantastic things he can do, with himself and with the world about him! What a summit nature has achieved in his creation! And yet if there is in man infinite capacity for good, there is also infinite capacity for evil. Every one of us has within himself the possibilities of both. I have long recognized within myself the potentiality for great evil—of the worst crime, just as I have within me the potentiality for great good. My mother used to say, "Every man has good and bad within him. He must make his choice. It is the choice that counts. You must hear the good in you and obey it."

When I was in my teens, the first major crisis developed

in my life. I cannot say what its precise causes were. I was nearing the end of my studies at the school, and my future was not yet really determined. I was intensely troubled by the continuing difference between my parents about my career. They had not yet resolved this disagreement. My father still felt it was foolhardy for me to think of devoting myself to a musical career; my mother was determined that I should. The thought that I was the cause of this dissension pained me deeply. I longed for it to be ended. Meanwhile, my mind was teeming with new ideas, new concepts and thoughts, constantly exploring, searching and examining the world about me. My horizons had greatly expanded; I read everything I could get my hands on, and thought more and more about the meaning of life. Before, I had found so much of beauty. Yet now how much ugliness there was that I saw! How much evil! How much pain and human travail! I would ask myself: Was man created to live in such squalor and degradation? All about me I saw evidence of suffering, of poverty, of misery, of man's inhumanity to man. I saw people who lived in hunger and had almost nothing to feed their children. I saw beggars in the streets and the age-old inequality of the rich and the poor. I became a witness to the oppression that simple people endured in their lives, and to harsh laws and repressive measures. Injustice and violence revolted me. I shuddered at the sight of an officer with his sword. Day and night I brooded on these conditions. I walked the streets of Barcelona feeling sick and full of apprehension. I was in a pit of darkness, at odds with the world. I dreaded the dawning of the day, and at night I sought escape in sleep. I could not understand why there was such evil in the world, why men should do such things to one another, or what, indeed, was the purpose of life under such circumstances—or of my own existence. Selfishness was rampant; and where, I asked myself, was compassion to be found?

I could no longer lose myself in my music. I did not feel then—nor have I ever felt—that music, or any form of art, can be an answer in itself. Music must serve a purpose; it must be a part of something larger than itself, a part of humanity; and that, indeed, is at the core of my argument with music today—its lack of humanity. A musician is also a man, and more important than his music is his attitude toward life. Nor can the two be separated.

The anguish in me became such that I thought perhaps the only way in which I could put an end to my torment was to put an end to myself. I became obsessed with the idea of suicide. I did not tell my mother that I had thoughts of killing myself. I could not give her that anxiety. But she—looking at me—sensed my inner agony; she could always see what was inside me. "What is it?" she would say to me. "What is it, dear Pablo, that is troubling you so?" I would say, "It is nothing, dear Mother." She would be silent; she did not probe; but I could see the apprehension and pain in her eyes.

Something in me, some innate will to live, some deep *élan vital* perhaps, fought against my killing myself. There was a war within me. I sought other avenues of escape, of respite. Perhaps, I thought, I could find solace in religion. I spoke of religion to my mother. She herself was not religious in a formal sense; she never went to Mass. Ordinarily she did not talk about religion, though I never heard her say anything against another person's religion or faith. She respected the beliefs of others. She did not try to influence me in this regard. She said to me, "This is something you must find for yourself, my son. You have everything within yourself, dear Pablo. You must find yourself." I turned to religious mysticism. I would go to a church near school after my classes, and I would sit there in the shadows, trying to lose myself in prayer, trying desperately to find consolation and an answer to my questions, searching for calm and

Casals as a youth, shortly before leaving Barcelona in 1894 to study in Madrid

some easement of the torment afflicting me. I would leave the church, go a few steps, then hurry back to it. But it was to no avail. And failing to find an answer in man's dreams of heaven, I sought for one in the panaceas he dreamed of on earth. I had read some of the writings of Karl Marx and Engels; and there were socialists among my friends. I thought that in the doctrine of socialism I might find an answer. It was not so—here too I found a dogma that could not satisfy me and a utopian dream that was unreal to me. It was full of illusions about changing society and man. And how, I asked myself, is man to be changed when he is full of selfishness and cynicism, when aggression is part of his nature?

It is difficult to say what brought me out of the abyss. Perhaps the inner struggle and love of life, the hope in me that would not be destroyed. Then, too, about this time my mother—who gave me every support in this hour of my great need—decided that the time had come for me to leave Barcelona. Though I had not confided in her the depths of my despair, she sensed it. That was when she proposed our going to Madrid. "The time has come," she said, "for us to take Albéniz's advice and to use his letter of introduction to the Count de Morphy."

There were long and agitated conversations between my mother and my father. He was full of misgivings. There was also the question of my mother's taking along my brothers, Luis and Enrique—they had both been born while we were in Barcelona. Luis was about three and Enrique was still an infant. But in the end it was decided that my mother and I and the two children would go. What would have happened to me if I had not gone to Madrid at that time, I do not know.

iv

Madrid

To be a teacher is to have a great responsibility. The teacher helps shape and give direction to the lives of other human beings. What is more important, graver, than that? Children and young people are our greatest treasure; when we think of them we think of the future of the world. Then consider the significance of nurturing their minds, of helping form their outlook on the world, of training and preparing them for the work that they will do. I can think of no profession more important than that of teaching. A good teacher, a true teacher, can be like a second father to his pupil. And this was the role that the Count de Morphy was to assume in my life. His influence was second only to that of my mother.

The Count Guillermo de Morphy was like many men in one; he had so many talents, abilities and skills. His mind encompassed a vast area of knowledge. He had, you might say, the versatility and *Weltanschauung* of a Renaissance man. He was a scholar and a historian, an author and a musician, a counselor to royalty and a composer, a patron of the arts and a poet. His interests embraced art and litera-ture, politics and philosophy, science and society, and, above all, music. He was especially interested in the work

of young musicians and befriended many of them—Albéniz, Granados, Tomás Bretón and others were among his
protégés. Together with the great Catalan musicologist,
Felipe Pedrell, he helped bring about a rebirth in Spanish
music. His great love was the opera. He was the founder of
the modern Spanish opera; he sought to free it from the
Italian influence, and restore the true national character to
its music. How he loved the music of Spain and how much
he knew about it! He wrote a magnificent book about the
history of Spanish music, dealing with great composers
from the fifteenth through the nineteenth century—the
book still serves as a text for students of Spanish music. He
pioneered in the study of the history of the lute in Spain;
in fact, he devoted twenty-five years to the study of old
Spanish lute tablatures; and he wrote a monumental classic
work entitled *Les Luthistes Espagnols du XVI Siècle*—it
was, sadly enough, not published until after his death.

The count had been the private tutor of King Alfonso
XII. When I met him he was an aide and personal secretary
to the Queen Regent María Cristina. At court the grandees
referred to him, somewhat contemptuously, as *el músico*,
"the musician." Their attitude was of course a commentary
on their limitations, not his.

There was a curious sidelight to the background of this
splendid man who knew so much about the national music
of Spain and exerted such an influence on its reassertion:
he himself was not of Spanish ancestry. He was the grandson of an Irishman who had been exiled from Ireland for his
political activities. The name of the Count de Morphy derived from *Murphy!*

On a wall in my house at San Salvador—in a room I call
the "Room of Sentiment"—there hangs a treasured possession of mine. It is a photograph of the Count de Morphy.
Inscribed on it, in verse, are these words:

I ask the Lord to testify
To Pablito that I do not lie
But stand in Heaven's grace
When now I do contend
The features of this ugly face
Are those of his best friend.

Yes, he was more than my teacher, patron and guide. He was my best friend.

When my mother and I—with my two young brothers, Luis and Enrique—arrived in Madrid on that fateful day in 1894, I was seventeen years old. We went immediately to see the Count de Morphy at his house in the suburb Barrio de Argüello. It was the home of a man of true distinction —that is, a man distinguished in culture and taste. Every piece of furniture in that house, every antique, rug and painting, had been selected with care and affection. When you entered his drawing room and saw his beautiful piano and musical scores, you *felt* the music in the man. His library was marvelous, with hundreds of books—old and new—on every imaginable subject. He was a rather small man in his late fifties, immaculately groomed, with a neatly trimmed beard, high forehead and thinning hair. He had a gracious, unpretentious, very gentle manner. He welcomed us with great warmth, and as soon as he had read Albéniz's letter, he asked if I had brought any of my compositions to Madrid with me. I had brought along a bundle of them, including a string quartet I had written when I was fourteen or fifteen. "Will you play for me?" he asked. I did. When I had finished, he said, "Yes, you are an artist, Pablito."

The count made an appointment for me to play at the Royal Palace for the Infanta Isabel. She was the sister of King Alfonso XII, and she had a great interest in music. It was an unforgettable occasion for me, not only because it

A Dios pongo por testigo,
porque Pablito me crea,
que es esta cara tan fea
la de su mejor amigo   G Morphy   noviembre 1898

Casals' tutor, patron and mentor, Count Guillermo de Morphy

was the first time I had ever played—or, for that matter, been—in a palace. My mother had nowhere to leave my two small brothers, and so she brought them along. Enrique was still an infant, and while I was playing one of my compositions for the infanta, he began to cry. That is, of course, a natural thing for a hungry infant to do, even when he is in a palace. Enrique was a lusty little boy and his crying made quite a noise, which contended with my music. Quietly, without any fuss or the slightest show of embarrassment, my mother unfastened her dress and proceeded to nurse Enrique. I continued playing. . . . I do not know whether such an episode had ever happened before during a musical performance at the palace, or whether it was *comme il faut* with court protocol. But this was a question that made no difference to my mother. She would have fed Enrique anywhere else—so why not in the Palace with the infanta seated nearby? She was not at all impressed by the fact that she was in the presence of royalty. The infanta to her was no different from any other person. That was the way my mother was.

Shortly afterwards, the count presented my mother and me to the queen regent. She received us very graciously and arranged for me to play in a concert at the palace. I appeared at that concert as both a performer and a composer. One of the works performed was my first string quartet, and I played the cello part.

The next morning the count had important and exciting news for my mother and me. The queen, he told us, had decided to give me a scholarship. It amounted to 250 pesetas —about $50.00—a month. That was not such a small amount then—in fact, it was quite a handsome sum in those days. Even so, it was not a great deal when it came to meeting the needs of a family of four. We lived very poorly.

My mother found us a room—it was really a garret on

the top floor of a house on the Calle San Quintín opposite the palace. Our room overlooked the palace gardens with their old statues of kings. There were four other apartments on the floor, and our neighbors on the landing were all working people, fine people, boisterous and companionable. They took a special interest in the fact that a young man who played the cello had arrived in their midst, and they quickly became friends with my mother, who was always ready to go out of her way to help anyone. One of our neighbors was a hall porter at the palace; he was especially proud of his uniform, and he used to wear it all the time— sometimes I wondered if he slept in it! Also, there were a shoemaker and his family—the poor man had two mentally retarded children. And there were several women who worked at the trade of making cigars. The place was in a constant hubbub, with youngsters running about, children crying and mothers scolding them, husbands and wives quarreling, shouts and songs and arguments that went on into the early morning hours. What confusion! What a din! But I didn't let it interfere with my work. I must, in fact, admit that I added to the many sounds, because I was constantly practicing on my cello. . . .

I began a program of intensive study under the tutelage of the Count de Morphy. He saw that there were many gaps in my education and that I had much to learn if I was to go out into the world as an artist. Each morning I would go to his house at nine o'clock and work steadily with him for the next three hours. That period was devoted to what one might call general education. Then we would lunch together with his wife and his stepdaughter. The countess—a lovely woman and a talented musician herself who had been a pupil of Liszt—gave me lessons in German. After lunch the count would have me improvise at the piano and would criticize my improvisations. One comment of his stays with me always. When I indulged in some particularly intricate harmony, for which I then had a certain fondness, he would put his arm about my shoulders—he always sat beside me on the piano stool—and say, gently, "Pablito, in the language of everybody—yes?" In the language of everybody! Of course, what more profound utterance could there be on the purpose of art in general? What purpose, indeed, can music—or any form of art—serve if it does not speak in a language that all can understand?

The count's teachings, as I have indicated, were by no means confined to musical subjects. He undertook to teach me everything he could about life and the world in which I lived—language and literature; art and geography; philosophy and mathematics; the history of music, yes, but also the history of man. The count contended that in order to be a fully developed artist, one had to have a full understanding of life. He regarded art and life as intimately interrelated. They cannot be separated, he would say. He was not only a man of rare gifts but a philosopher of high intelligence.

He had me visit the Prado museum regularly. Before I went, he would tell me, "Pablito, today you should study one of Velásquez's paintings." Or it might be a painting by Murillo, Titian or Goya. In the corridors and halls of that massive imposing building, I would stand before the paintings, examining the artist's technique, musing on the meaning of his work. "What is he saying?" I would ask myself. "How has he managed to achieve the effect?" Then I would submit to the count an essay on the painting, and we would discuss what I had written.

Once a week he sent me to the Cortes to listen in the Senate or the Chamber of Deputies to the speeches and the debates of the leading politicians and orators of the day. Then I would write for him a report on what I had heard and observed.

My mother studied too while I was studying. She studied not only foreign languages but other subjects as well. She did this not only to help me with my work but also to keep any gap from developing between us in our education.

Many of the textbooks that the count used with me were the same ones he had used with King Alfonso XII. In the margins of these books I would frequently come upon the king's notations. The count used to say, "I have had two sons—Alfonso and Pablito." I came to address him as "Papá."

How understanding and tender he was with me! Sometimes at lunch, when he saw I was preoccupied or sad— during the early part of my stay in Madrid I was still recovering from the depression that had afflicted me in Barcelona—he would tell humorous stories and witty jokes to amuse me, with his bright eyes twinkling. And often he managed to make me laugh.

The count carried on my private instruction for two and a half years. He was not appointed to do this. He had made the decision entirely on his own. What a debt I owe to that great and good man!

During the time the count was tutoring me, I was studying also at the Madrid Conservatory of Music. The count had arranged for me to study composition with Tomás Bretón, then one of the most important composers in Spain. His operas were very much in vogue at the time—the count took me to hear the first performance of his famous work, *La Verbena de la Paloma.*

Jesús de Monasterio, the director of the conservatory, was my teacher in chamber music. Monasterio was a brilliant violinist, a prodigy who had received royal patronage at the age of seven. He was a magnificent teacher. I could not have had a better teacher at this formative stage of my career. I would say that next to my father he was the greatest musical influence upon my life. How much he did to open my eyes and ears to the true inner meaning of music and to teach me about style! I had already developed a compulsion for accurate intonation—it was something that musicians paid little attention to at the time; but Monasterio reinforced my convictions in the matter. He also encouraged my work on musical accentuation, to which I attached great importance. His approach toward music was a profoundly serious one. It was the *fin-de-siècle* period—artists with flowing hair, flowing ties and flowing words! Elaborate flourishes, mannerisms and melodramatics were the fashion of the hour. But not with Monasterio. He placed great emphasis on the underlying principles of music—he never regarded music as a toy, a whim. For him music was an expression of man's dignity and nobility.

When I became his pupil, Monasterio was about sixty years old. A deeply considerate man, he treated me with great affection. Sometimes in class when he would talk about the laws of music—for him, music was a language, with similar laws of accent and values and constant variety —or when he would give examples on his violin, he would look at me out of the corner of his eye, as if to say, "You understand me!"

One day he told the class we must all be sure to come the following day. He said, "We have a pupil who has so distinguished himself that the queen is conferring an honor upon him. Tomorrow you will know his name." The next day I learned he had been referring to me. It was from his hand that I received my first decoration from Queen María Cristina, my protector. It was the Medal of the Order of Isabel la Católica. I was eighteen at the time.

I was a frequent visitor at the palace. I would go there two or three times a week to play the cello, improvise at the piano or perform in concerts. I came to be treated as if I

Casals' teacher, the director of the Madrid Conservatory of Music
and eminent violinist, Jesús de Monasterio. The inscription reads:
"To the distinguished artist and greatly valued friend, Pablo Casals,
his old master, J. de Monasterio, Santander—August 1900"

were a member of the royal family. Queen María Cristina, who was a good pianist, often played duets with me. We sat at the same piano and played together, four hands. She was a gracious, sensitive woman; and she was immensely kind to me. I grew greatly attached to her. She became not only my patron but a second mother to me.

It was then too that I first came to know King Alfonso XIII. He was seven years old, a dear boy! We became very fond of each other, and he liked me to tell him stories. He had a passion for toy soldiers and we used to play with them together—lining up his little troops in marches and maneuvers. I would bring him stamps and he would sit on my knee. I have never lost my affection for the royal family or forgotten my indebtedness to them.

But this, of course, was a personal matter. It had nothing to do with my feelings about the monarchy or about court life in general. That was a world to which I felt I did not belong and which I did not like. There was much affectation among the nobility, with their airs and pretensions; and there was constant court intrigue. I had grown up among the common people, and I continued to identify myself with them. I was by upbringing and inclination a Republican. Then, too, I was a Catalan and deeply proud of the fact; and Castilian aristocrats tended to look down upon the Catalans.

Years later when Alfonso was the ruling monarch, I once told him, "You are the king, and I love you, but I am a Republican." He said, "Of course, you are. I know that. It is your right." And how could it be otherwise? True, I am an artist, but in the practice of my art I am also a manual worker. This I have been all my life. And so, when there would finally come a choice between the monarchy and the Republic, it was inevitable my sympathies would be with the Republic. . . .

My association with the members of the royal family of

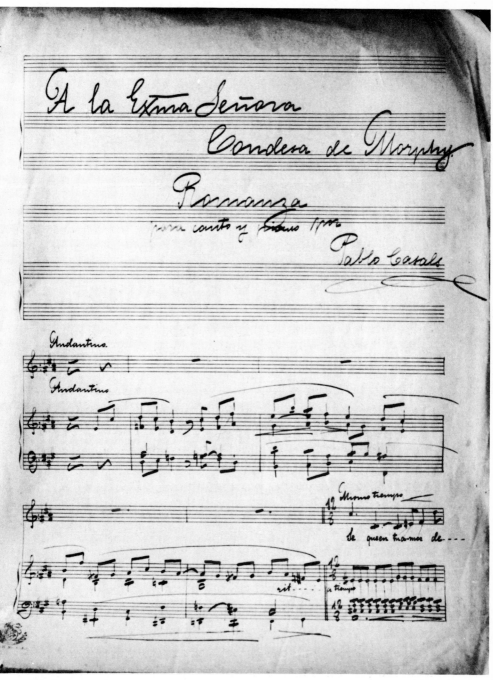

The score of a composition dedicated by the young Casals to the
Countess de Morphy, while he was studying in Madrid with the count

Spain, however, would continue over the years. Indeed, my most recent contact took place more than seventy years after my first visit to the palace in Madrid. It occurred in the summer of 1966 when I went to Greece to conduct a performance of my peace oratorio, *El Pessebre*. There, in Athens, I saw Juan Carlos, the grandson of Alfonso XIII. I congratulated him for not accepting the crown under Franco. I told him, "I have known five generations of Spanish royalty, beginning with Isabel II." Juan Carlos, who had married the Greek princess, Sophia, came the following day with his wife to my hotel. They brought with them their two-year-old daughter. And so I came to know the sixth generation.

How regrettable it is that Juan Carlos has recently pledged to carry on as Franco's heir in Spain! And how different was the attitude of the exiled king, his grandfather, to this regime!

I had been in Madrid for almost three years when my mother said she thought that I had spent enough time on my studies there and the time had come for a change. I should now concentrate on playing the cello, she said. I agreed with her. She suggested the possibility of our returning to Barcelona. When the count heard this proposal, he was very much opposed to it. He wanted me to remain in Madrid and work with him. He wanted me to become a composer. I would be a protégé of his in the opera. My mother's views were very different. "I believe," she told the count, "that with Pablo the cello comes before everything else. If his future is to be that of a composer, it can always come later, and his work on the cello won't interfere. But if he fails to concentrate on the instrument now, it will prove a serious disadvantage later." The disagreement became intense. The debate between them went on for weeks, and the situation became very strained. The queen too was against my leaving. And my father was greatly disturbed by these developments. "What do you have in mind?" he wrote my mother. "What on earth will come of this?" But my mother was adamant.

Finally a compromise solution was reached. The count agreed to my leaving Madrid on one condition—that I go to study music at the Conservatory of Music in Brussels. It was then the best music conservatory in Europe and offered excellent instruction not only in composition but also in stringed instruments. The count said that I could study composition there under François Gevaert, the director of the conservatory, a renowned figure in the musical world who was an old friend of his. The count told my mother and me that he would make arrangements with the queen for my pension of 250 pesetas a month to continue while I was at the conservatory. The matter was settled, and we left for Brussels. Enrique and Luis went with us. Before our departure, the count gave us a letter of introduction to Gevaert.

I have spent many happy hours of my life in Brussels, but my first visit there was not among them. It was not an auspicious occasion. The trip across France in the crowded third-class compartment of the train seemed endless, and when we finally arrived in Brussels—it was the first time I had ever set foot in a foreign land—what I saw depressed me. How different it was from sunny Catalonia! The time was winter. I hate the cold, and it was cold, damp and miserable. A fog hung over the city.

We went straightway to the Conservatory of Music to see François Gevaert. He was a noted musicologist and historian with a very interesting career. He came of humble origins—his father was a baker and wanted him to follow the trade, but his musical talents soon asserted themselves. As a young man, he won a wide reputation for his compositions—church music and operas. He traveled in Spain and became an authority on Spanish music. For a while he was director of music at the Paris Opéra, and then he began devoting his attention to the history of music. He was a great scholar. He wrote many works. One of them was the classic *Histoire et Théorie de la Musique de l'Antiquité.* He had a great influence on the Count de Morphy's career and encouraged his study of the history of the lute in Spain. Shortly before Gevaert's death, this baker's son was made a baron by the Belgian king to honor him for his composition of a national hymn for the Congo.

I gave Gevaert the letter from the Count de Morphy. He was an elderly man, quite frail, with a long white beard. He read the letter slowly and carefully. We talked about the count, Madrid and music. He asked to see some of my compositions. I had brought with me a mass that I had composed, a symphonic poem, and a string quartet. He expressed surprise at my technique. "But I am sorry," he said, "I am very sorry. I am really too old now to give lessons in composition, and from what I see here, I don't think I could teach you very much." He said, "What you need most of all is to hear music, to hear all the music you can, to attend musical performances of all sorts. Brussels is not the place for that. The center of music today is Paris. That is where you must go. There you will hear the best symphony orchestras in the world—there are four orchestras there, Lamoureux, Colonne, Padelou, and the Conservatory of Music. You will hear everything. And that is what you need." He added that the count's letter had mentioned my abilities as a cellist. "I'd like our cello professor here at the conservatory to hear you play," he said. "Could you come tomorrow morning?"

The next day I appeared at the class. I was very nervous because of the conservatory's reputation as the best school in the world for stringed instruments. I sat in the back of the class, listening to the students play. I must say I was not too greatly impressed, and I began to feel less nervous. When the class had finished, the professor—who until then had given no sign he had noticed my presence—beckoned to me. "So," he said, "I gather you're the little Spaniard that the director spoke to me about." I did not like his tone.

I said yes, that I was the one.

"Well, little Spaniard," he said, "it seems you play the cello. Do you wish to play?"

I said I would be glad to.

"And what compositions do you play?"

I said I played quite a few.

He rattled off a number of works, asking me each time if I could play the one he named, and each time I said yes —because I could. Then he turned to the class and said, "Well now, isn't that remarkable! It seems that our young Spaniard plays everything. He must be really quite amazing."

The students laughed. At first I had been upset by the professor's manner—this was, after all, my second day in a strange country—but by now I was angry with the man and his ridicule of me. I didn't say anything.

"Perhaps," he said, "you will honor us by playing the *Souvenir de Spa?*" It was a flashy piece that was trotted out regularly in the Belgian school.

I said I would play it.

"I'm sure we'll hear something astonishing from this young man who plays everything," he said. "But what will you use for an instrument?"

There was more laughter from the students.

I was so furious I almost left then and there. But I thought, all right, whether he wants to hear me play or not, he'll hear me. I snatched a cello from the student nearest to me, and I began to play. The room fell silent. When I had finished, there wasn't a sound.

The professor stared at me. His face had a strange expression. "Will you please come to my office?" he said. His tone was very different than before. We walked from the room together. The students sat without moving.

The professor closed the door to his office and sat down behind his desk. "Young man," he said, "I can tell you that you have a great talent. If you study here, and if you consent to be in my class, I can promise you that you will be awarded the First Prize of the conservatory. Mind you, it's not exactly according to regulations for me to tell you this at this time, but I can give you my word."

I was almost too angry to speak. I told him, "You were rude to me, sir. You ridiculed me in front of your pupils. I do not want to remain here one second longer."

He stood up—his face was white—and he opened the door for me.

The very next day we left for Paris. As soon as we arrived there, I wrote the Count de Morphy and told him exactly what had happened in Brussels and why we had come to Paris. His reply showed his annoyance. I had disobeyed him, he said—our understanding had been that I was to go not to Paris but to study at the Brussels conservatory. "Your pension from the queen," he said, "was extended on that understanding. That is what the queen wants. And unless you return to Brussels, your pension will be discontinued." I wrote back saying that Brussels simply was not the place for me, and that, although I did not want to go against his wishes, I planned to stay in Paris. His answer indicated he was convinced I had come to Paris because of my mother's influence; but it was not so. I myself knew there was no purpose in returning to Brussels.

My pension from the queen was promptly cut off.

Those were trying days in Paris! We had counted on the pension, and without it we were virtually stranded—my mother, my two young brothers and I. We had no means of support. What were we to do? My father, who now of course worried more than ever about us, could afford to send us practically nothing.

My mother found us living quarters in what was little more than a hovel near the Porte St.-Denis. It was a very depressing neighborhood—poverty was all about us. My mother began going out every day to try to earn some money. Where she went I don't know; she used to come back with things to sew. There was barely enough for the little ones to eat.

I too of course was trying desperately to find work. Finally I got a job as a second cellist at a music hall called the Folies-Marigny on the Champs-Élysées. It was the time when Toulouse-Lautrec was painting in Paris; and now, when I look at his paintings, I think of that music hall and of the dancers doing the cancan, which was then very much the fashion. I earned four francs a day. I walked to and from the Folies-Marigny carrying my cello—it was far from where we lived, but the tramway fare was fifteen centimes, and we did not have a sou to spare.

It was a bitterly cold winter. At last the strain of the work and the lack of food proved too much. I became very ill and had to stay home. My mother worked harder than ever, to feed us and buy the medicines I needed. She sewed late into the nights. She was always cheerful and did everything to keep up my spirits.

Then one day, when she came home and I was lying sick in bed, I hardly recognized her; I realized something extraordinary had happened to her. Looking at her in astonishment and dismay, I saw that she no longer had her beautiful, long, black hair. Her hair was now ragged and short. She had sold her hair to get a few extra francs for us.

She laughed about it. "Never mind," she said. "Don't think about it. It is only hair, and hair grows back."

But I was sick at heart.

Our ordeal continued. Finally I said, "Mother, how can we go on this way? Why don't we go back to Barcelona?"

"All right," she said, "let us go back to Barcelona."

And so we returned.

My father—he had been able to visit us only once during our prolonged absence in Madrid—was overjoyed to have us back. However, he was dismayed at the turn in our fortunes. The family's small savings had vanished.

But I did not feel discouraged. I had my mother's example before me.

V

Firm Soil

That splendid Catalan poet, Joan Maragall, once wrote, "To take flight to Heaven, we must stand on the firm soil of our native land." Catalonia is my native land. I had been gone for almost three years, and it was a joy for me to be back.

During my lifetime, I have traveled in many lands, and I have found beauty everywhere. But the beauty of Catalonia nourished me since infancy. And when I close my eyes, I see the ocean at San Salvador and the seaside village of Sitges with the little fishing boats on the sand, the vineyards and olive groves and pomegranate trees of the province of Tarragona, the River Llobregat and the peaks of Montserrat. Catalonia is the land of my birth, and I love her as a mother. . . .

I am, of course, a Spanish citizen. Though I have lived in exile for more than thirty years, I still carry a Spanish passport. I could not dream of parting with it. An official at the Spanish consulate at Perpignan once asked me why I did not relinquish my passport if I chose not to return to Spain. I replied, "Why should I give it up? Let Franco give up his. And then I shall return." But first and foremost I am a Catalan. Since I have felt this way for almost a century, I do not expect to change.

We Catalans have our own national language—it is an ancient Romance language, completely distinct from Castilian Spanish. We have our own culture—the sardana is our dance, and what a lovely dance it is! And we have our own history. Already in the Middle Ages, Catalonia was a great nation, and her influence reached into France and Italy—even today in both countries you will find many people still speaking Catalan. We had no kings—we were satisfied to have counts as our rulers. And in our Constitution in the Middle Ages were these words that the Catalan people had addressed to their ruler: "Each of us is equal to you, and together all of us are greater than you." As early as the eleventh century, Catalonia summoned a convocation that called for the abolishment of war in the world. What better evidence of a high civilization could there be than that?

All nations have a diminuendo. Not many years ago it was said that the sun never set on the British Empire; today England remains, but her empire is no more. Catalonia too is not the powerful nation she once was. But that does not diminish her history or justify the denial of her national rights. Yet Catalonia has become little more than a Spanish subject. We Catalans want to live with the other peoples of Spain as brothers—not as servants, which is what happens under the present Spanish regime. We are forbidden in our public schools to teach our native tongue; instead, Castilian is taught. Our culture is stifled.

I have always been opposed to extreme nationalism. The people of no one nation are superior to those of any other —different, yes, but superior, no. Extreme nationalists believe they have the right to dominate other nations. Patriotism is something wholly different. Love of one's soil is deep in the nature of man. I think of the death of Luis Companys. I came to know Companys when he was President of Catalonia during the days of the Spanish Republic. There were matters in which I disagreed with Companys, but he was a patriot. He had been a brilliant lawyer who championed the cause of the Catalan working people. When the fascists seized power, Companys was among the Republican leaders who escaped to France. Franco demanded he be sent back, and the Pétain government obliged. The Spanish fascists executed him. When he faced the firing squad, Companys lit a cigarette and then he removed his shoes and socks. He wanted to die with his feet touching the soil of Catalonia.

In Barcelona, my fortunes underwent a sudden change. The difficult days of Paris, with all their privations and uncertainties, soon receded into the past. My old friend and teacher, Josep García, who had introduced me to the wonders of the cello when I was a boy of eleven, had just resigned from his professorship at the Municipal School of Music—he was about to go to live in Argentina. I was invited to fill his post at the school. At the same time, it was arranged for me to take over the instruction of García's private pupils and his engagements to play at church services. Before many months had passed, I was also asked to teach at the Liceu School of Music, and I was appointed principal cellist in the opera orchestra. Suddenly, I had more work than I could handle!

My work as a teacher now absorbed most of my time. It was an important period in my maturing as a musician. I have never drawn an artificial line between teaching and learning. A teacher, of course, should know more than his pupil. But for me, to teach is to learn. It was so for me then at the Municipal School of Barcelona; and it remains so for me today.

I continued to work on the development of my technique.

I was determined not to be hampered by any of the restrictions of the past—to learn from the past but not be shackled by it. My aim was to achieve the best possible effects on the cello. I have always regarded technique as a means, not an end in itself. One must, of course, master techniques; at the same time, one must not become enslaved by it—one must understand that the purpose of technique is to transmit the inner meaning, the message, of the music. The most perfect technique is that which is not noticed at all. I constantly asked myself, "What is the most natural way of doing this?" I taught my pupils the methods of fingering and bowing that I had begun to develop when I was a student at the Municipal School. I taught the importance of relaxation—cello playing demands such tension in the left hand that one must constantly exercise it to maintain flexibility. I showed my pupils how, at certain moments, it was possible to relax the hand and the arm—if only for a fraction of a second—while performing. Above all, I emphasized that the most important thing is to have respect for the music and to understand the great responsibility the artist has in bringing a composer's music to life.

There is of course no substitute for work. I myself practiced constantly, as I have all my life. I have been told I play the cello with the ease of a bird flying. I do not know with how much effort a bird learns to fly, but I do know what effort has gone into my cello. What seems ease of performance comes from the greatest labor. There are, of course, exceptions, as with my friend Albéniz, who never practiced. But such cases are rarities. Almost always, facility results only from maximum effort. Art is the product of labor.

When summer came, my work in Barcelona slackened off. I had no classes at the Municipal School, and other jobs were temporarily discontinued. So when I received the offer

of an engagement at a casino at Espinho, a resort south of
Oporto on the coast of Portugal, I readily accepted it. My
route lay through Madrid, and I thought how wonderful it
would be if I could see the Count de Morphy again. I still
felt unhappy about the misunderstanding that had arisen
between us the year before when I had gone to Paris. I
wrote the count a letter relating everything that had happened and telling him of the engagement I now had in Espinho. Would he like to see me, I asked, when I came
through Madrid? I awaited his answer anxiously. "Come as
soon as possible," he wrote back. It was characteristic of
his gentleness and understanding.

The moment I arrived in Madrid, I hurried to his house.
He welcomed me as a son. We talked and talked—it was as
if there had never been any difficulty between us.

In Madrid I also saw Queen María Cristina. She greeted
me with great warmth and made me tell her all the details
of my adventures since we had last seen each other. She
was deeply affected when I described the trials my mother
and I had endured in Paris, and she was delighted to know
about the work I was now carrying on in Barcelona. She
asked me to play for her at the palace. After the recital, she
took me aside. "Pablo," she said, "I want to give you something that you can always keep as a remembrance of me. I
want it to be something you can touch." She pointed to an
exquisite bracelet she was wearing. "Which of these stones
do you like best?" she asked.

I was almost too moved to answer. "They are all so beautiful, Your Majesty," I told her.

"Then you shall have this one," she said, singling out a
magnificent sapphire.

Later, I had the stone mounted in my bow as a cherished
memento of that most gracious woman whom I remember
with love.

From Madrid I went to Espinho. The casino, an ornately furnished establishment overlooking the sea, was mainly a gambling place where Portuguese aristocrats, wealthy merchants and other fashionable folk came to wile away their summer days. The management wanted to keep them happy—perhaps in case their losings were too great—with pleasant music. There was dancing too, of course. We had a septet, and, as at the Café Tost, I played a solo once a week. We played in a café adjoining the gambling room. Word about the concerts spread, and music lovers started coming to the casino from all parts of Portugal. Toward the end of the season, to my considerable surprise, I received an invitation from the King and Queen of Portugal to visit them at their palace. I hurriedly packed and took the train to Lisbon. When I arrived at the palace, King Carlos and Queen Marie-Amélie received me most cordially. "And will you play for us?" they inquired. At that point I realized I hadn't brought my cello with me! I said, "Yes, I shall be glad to play . . . only I have no cello. I left it at the hotel in Espinho." They laughed good-naturedly at my embarrassment. My cello was sent for, and I played the following day. That was the only occasion in my musical career when I arrived for a recital without my cello.

I was to return to the palace in Lisbon several years later with my dear friend, the pianist Harold Bauer. He was, I remember, greatly impressed with the beauty of Queen Marie-Amélie, who was a very striking-looking woman. He was also impressed with her height—she was more than six feet tall. He commented to me afterwards on the difference between her size and mine—I have never been much taller than my cello. I told him, "It's not that I'm too small; it's that the queen's too tall."

At the end of the summer, on my way home, I stopped again in Madrid. On that visit I played my first concert as a soloist with an orchestra. I played the Lalo Concerto in D Minor. My former teacher, Tomás Bretón, conducted, and many friends from my student days in Madrid attended the performance. Again I visited the Count de Morphy and Queen María Cristina. The queen presented me with a superb Gagliano cello. She also conferred on me a decoration —the second she had given me; the first had been when I was a pupil at the Royal Conservatory. This time she gave me the Order of Carlos III. It was a high honor for a youth of twenty, but I regarded it especially as a mark of her personal affection and her faith in me.

Following my return to Barcelona, some fellow musicians and I formed a string quartet, and we began giving chamber music recitals in Valencia, Madrid and other cities. The other members of the quartet were the eminent Belgian violinist Mathieu Crickboom, who had settled in Barcelona, the violist Galvez, and the pianist and composer Enrique Granados. Granados and I had become close friends—I had conducted the rehearsals at the Liceu of his first opera, *María del Carmen*, when he himself felt too nervous to do so. Granados, who was in his late twenties when we met, was already recognized as one of the most talented musicians in Spain. The son of an army officer, he had received his first music lessons from the local bandmaster in the town of Lérida, where he had been born. Later he had studied with the renowned musicologist and composer Felipe Pedrell, who had rediscovered much of the Spanish folk music of earlier centuries and, together with the Count de Morphy, worked to create a true Spanish opera. Though Pedrell had a major influence on many young composers, Granados was actually almost entirely self-taught, and his exquisite and poetic compositions—which so embody the spirit of Spain—were largely the fruit of his own special genius. He

Casals (right) and his friend, the composer and pianist Enrique Granados, when they were colleagues in Barcelona before the turn of
the century

was a wonderful, natural pianist, and he had a remarkable habit: in the middle of a work by Beethoven, Schubert or some other great composer, it did not matter who, he would suddenly decide to improvise and would proceed to do so without the slightest hesitation! He was a lovely man, and a lovely-looking man, with large dark eyes, dark wavy hair, and the face of a poet. Our friendship, which was so precious to me, lasted until his untimely death twenty years later.

Playing with Granados was a source of much happiness to me. I have always preferred not to play as a soloist. I prefer playing sonatas or any other form of chamber music. For one thing, I am much less nervous beforehand—I can share the responsibility with the others! What I like most is when I don't play at all but conduct!

Another musician I came to know in those days was that amazing violinist Pablo Sarasate. He was then in his fifties and for some time he had been the most famous virtuoso in Spain. Actually, we had met before. I first heard him play when I was a boy studying in Barcelona. Señor Tost, the proprietor of the café where I played, took me to one of Sarasate's performances, and I was overwhelmed by the brilliance of his playing—I had never heard anything like it. Later, when I was studying in Madrid, the Count de Morphy took me to meet Sarasate at the hotel where he was staying. He was very elegant, very debonair, with a long slender mustache, flowing black hair and gleaming black eyes. He smoked cigars incessantly. At one point during the conversation, he offered me some brandy. When I declined, he said, "What? You intend to be an artist, and you don't drink? Why, that's impossible!"

Sarasate played the violin with fantastic facility. His performances were dazzling, spectacular—like fireworks! He was a born showman, and when he played he would look straight at the audience as if saying, "See what I can do? Yes, I know you're spellbound!" He never practiced or prepared for a concert. He just came and played. He was a great violinist without being a great artist in the true sense of the word.

He was a very amusing man with a wry sense of humor, always making jokes. Sometimes he came with his friends the violinist Arbos and the cellist Rubio to stay at the casino in San Sebastian where I used to play in the summers. And every morning a little mock ceremony would take place when Arbos and Rubio went to see him in his room.

"Have I shown you my new cane?" Sarasate would say— he had a wonderful collection of canes, which he had accumulated on his travels around the world. Arbos and Rubio would say, "No, Pablo, we haven't seen the new one." He would get out of bed in his long nightshirt, stride over to the stand where he kept his canes and select one of them with a flourish. "Here it is. What a marvelous cane! Observe it closely. So strong—and yet so supple I can stretch it at will or bend it into a perfect circle." While he gestured with the cane, they watched with simulated wonder as if he were doing with it exactly what he said he was. "Another thing," he would say. "Really extraordinary, the way in which it responds to weather conditions. When the temperature falls you can see my initials on the cane, and when it rises they disappear. Look—today, because it's warmer, you can't see them at all!"

The ceremony would vary.

One morning when Arbos and Rubio asked Sarasate how he had slept, he threw up his arms and said with exasperation, "Sleep! How could I possibly sleep?"

"What do you mean, Pablo?"

"Well, how could anyone sleep in a room full of turtles?"

Program of a concert given by Casals, Enrique Granados and Mathieu
Crickboom at the Gran Casino Easonense in San Sebastian, Spain, 1897

Arbos and Rubio nodded understandingly, as if they were surrounded by turtles. "Ah yes, that is very disagreeable. . . ."

This same routine went on for several days. Then one morning, when Arbos and Rubio had asked the same question about how Sarasate had slept, and had received the same answer, they said, "You're right, Pablo. You really should complain. It's an impossible situation. Just look at them!" And they pointed around the room.

When Sarasate looked, he saw there were turtles crawling all around the room! Arbos and Rubio had come in the night and put them there.

But Sarasate didn't show any surprise. He just sighed with resignation and said, "You see how it is. . . ."

It was during this period when I was teaching in Barcelona that I formed a cherished association which would prove to be one of the most lasting of my lifetime. I came to know the monks at the monastery of Montserrat. I began visiting them frequently, and we engaged in long discussions about music, art, and a whole range of other matters. You might say that the monastery became like a second home to me.

The monastery is one of the most amazing institutions in the world. Its setting near Barcelona is fantastic. The name Montserrat, or "Serrated Mountain," comes from the shape of the mountain where the abbey is located—the jagged peaks cut into the sky like the spires of a mammoth cathedral. I know of no mountain anywhere more awesome and inspiring. The monastery is near the summit on a small plateau overlooking great ravines and precipices—its massive buildings seem rooted in the rocks. It was founded more than a thousand years ago, in the ninth century, when a statue of the Virgin Mary was discovered in a cave where

it had been hidden during the Moorish invasion of Catalonia. Later the monastery became a shrine to which
pilgrims journeyed from all parts of Europe to pay homage
to Our Lady of Montserrat, the patron saint of Catalonia.
Many people believed Montserrat was also the legendary
hiding place of the Holy Grail, the Montsalvat celebrated in
the songs of the troubadours and minnesingers of the Middle Ages. Not only religious music but folk music was part
of the monastery's life from its earliest days—the pilgrims
sang and danced in the square before the church, and the
monks themselves composed and arranged songs. As early
as the fourteenth century, the monks set down a group of
pilgrim songs in a volume known as the *Llibre Vermell*,
which is one of the earliest records of European polyphony.
Since the Middle Ages, the monks have continued to do
important work not only in musicology but in other
branches of art and learning. Among the monks themselves
there have been brilliant scholars, scientists, poets, musicians. How many unforgettable hours have I spent in the
company of the Benedictine brothers at Montserrat! To this
day we have not lost touch with one another.

Though their lives are dedicated to God, the monks of
Montserrat are deeply concerned with the affairs of men.
The abbey is a pillar of the Catalan heritage. Several years
ago the abbot, Father Escarré, a man of great wisdom and
gentle heart, was forced to leave Catalonia because of his
opposition to the Franco regime. He then went to live in
Milan. We continued to correspond regularly, and with one
of his letters he enclosed a lengthy interview he had given
the French newspaper *Le Monde;* it was entitled "Spain
Today Is Not a Christian Country." When the abbot recently died he was buried, as he had requested, in Catalonia
at Montserrat.

Despite Franco's edicts, the monks at Montserrat continued to perform marriage ceremonies and Masses in the Catalan language when its use was forbidden. In the darkest times they sang my works.

Over the years I have dedicated my religious compositions to the monastery. I have refrained from the publication of almost all my other works. The monks of Montserrat, however, have published my religious music. They sing my Masses regularly and my Rosary every day. . . .

Not long ago I was talking with a well-known young American musician. He is a fine musician with a real talent, but when I mentioned Montserrat, he did not know the name. "Montserrat?" he said. "He's a French painter, isn't he?" His question indicated something about contemporary musical education. Every musician should know the name of Montserrat. It is part of the heritage of the past without which the culture of the present would not be possible.

Throughout the period following my return to Barcelona from Paris, I avoided every extravagance and saved as much money as possible. I could not forget the hardships of those Paris days or the struggles of the previous years. I was determined to make life easier for my mother and father, who had sacrificed so much for me. Nothing gave me greater joy than being able to provide some comforts for my mother and two younger brothers, or to help my father get better care for his dreadful asthma. At the same time, I set aside such funds as I could to enable me to return to Paris and pursue my career there in the way that François Gevaert had envisioned.

By the summer of 1899 I was prepared. I discussed my plans with my parents, and they agreed the time had come for me to go back to France. When the well-known singer, Emma Nevada, invited me to visit her at her home near Paris—I had met her through the Count de Morphy—I

eagerly accepted the invitation. The story of Emma Nevada
—she was then in her late thirties—was like a romantic
novel. The name "Nevada" was adopted. Her father was an
American doctor who had gone to California during the
days of the Gold Rush—she had been born near the little
mining town of Nevada City and had later taken its name as
her stage sobriquet. At the time of her birth, California was
still the American frontier—the Civil War began when she
was two or three. Her childhood had been spent in a bizarre
world of gold prospectors, professional gamblers, and vigi-
lante committees. When she was eight years old, her parents had sent her to a seminary near San Francisco. She
showed a rare singing talent and came to England with a
traveling company at the age of fifteen. She made her opera
debut in London a few years later; it was a phenomenal
success, and she went from one triumph to another in the
capitals of Europe. She knew Verdi—he engaged her for
La Scala—and Gounod became her godfather.

When I arrived at Emma Nevada's home, she was about
to go to London to keep a singing engagement. She suggested I join her. It was my first trip to England. I was invited to perform at several musicales of society people who
in those days gave private concerts in their homes. Also, on
that visit, I made my London debut. I played the Saint-
Saëns concerto with an orchestra under the direction of the
conductor August Manns at the Crystal Palace—a huge
glass building where there was a permanent exposition with
all sorts of public entertainment besides music. When the
concert was over, I was introduced to a Mrs. Elliot, who was
lady in waiting to Queen Victoria. She asked me, "Would
you like to play for Her Majesty?" I said I would be happy
to do so.

The concert took place at Osborne House, the summer
residence of Queen Victoria on the Isle of Wight. It was a

handsome building, several hundred years old, surrounded by beautifully kept gardens. The atmosphere at the concert was much more formal than that to which I was accustomed at the Royal Palace in Madrid. There was an air of hushed solemnity in the rather small room in which the concert was held; and beforehand the guests—there were about thirty of them—conversed with one another in barely audible voices. Among those present to whom I was introduced were the Prince of Wales, who was soon to become King Edward VII, and the Duke of York, the future King George V. I was curious to meet Queen Victoria, who was then eighty and a legendary figure. She was a small stout woman with soft wrinkled cheeks and prominent eyes. She wore a headdress of white lace that came down to her shoulders. While she chatted with a British admiral, the rest of the guests stood about in respectful silence. An Indian servant in a green silk dress and yellow turban placed a stool under her feet, and she raised a small plump hand as a signal for the concert to begin. It did not last long. The pianist Walker accompanied me. We played, as I recall, three compositions, one of which was the Allegro from the Saint-Saëns concerto. There was no applause between the pieces, and at the end of the concert there was a polite clapping.

Queen Victoria, addressing me in French, congratulated me on my playing. She had, she said, heard about me from Queen María Cristina of Spain. She wished me success with my career and gave me several gifts. Before I left, the Duke of Connaught chatted briefly with me in Spanish and asked me to sign my name in a "Book of Honorable Guests."

Some time later when I was in Madrid, Queen María Cristina gave me as a present a telegram she had received from Queen Victoria following the concert. The telegram was in German. Queen Victoria said she had found my playing *entzüchend*—"delightful". . . .

Casals at the time of his Paris debut with the Lamoureux Orchestra
in 1899 at the age of twenty-two

THÉÂTRE DE LA RÉPUBLIQUE

SAISON 1899-1900   Ancien Théâtre du Château-d'Eau, 50, rue de Malte   19me ANNÉE

ASSOCIATION
DES
CONCERTS LAMOUREUX

Sous la Direction de **M. Charles LAMOUREUX**

Dimanche prochain 17 DÉCEMBRE 1899, à 2 h. 1/2

(Ouverture des portes à 1 h. 3/4)

SÉRIE B   **SIXIÈME CONCERT**   SÉRIE B

AVEC LE CONCOURS DE Mme

JANE MARCY
DE L'OPÉRA
ET DE M.

PABLO CASALS

PROGRAMME

SYMPHONIE *en ut mineur* (n° 5) . . . . . . **BEETHOVEN**

MUDARRA, Drame musical en 4 Actes, de MM. TIERCELIN et BONNEMÈRE . **F. LE BORNE**
  A. Prologue symphonique.
  B. Prélude et 1re Scène du 2me Acte.
  Mme Jane MARCY (de l'Opéra).

CONCERTO *pour Violoncelle* . . . . **SAINT-SAËNS**
  Par **M. PABLO CASALS.**

CAPRICCIO ESPAGNOL . . . . . **RIMSKY-KORSAKOW**
  Pour Orchestre.

AIR DE PROSERPINE . . . . **PAËSIELLO**
  Mme Jane MARCY (de l'Opéra).

OUVERTURE DE TANNHÄUSER . . . . . . **WAGNER**

PRIX DES PLACES : Avant-Scènes de Rez-de-Chaussée, **6 fr.**; Avant-Scènes de Balcon, **8 fr.**; Avant-Scènes de Première Galerie, **4 fr.**; Avant-Scènes de Deuxième Galerie, **2 fr.**; Fauteuils d'Orchestre, **8 fr.**; Loges de Balcon, **8 fr.**; Fauteuils de Balcon (1re série), **8 fr.**; Fauteuils de Balcon (2me série), **6 fr.**; Fauteuils de Foyer, **5 fr.**; Stalles de Deuxième Galerie, **3 fr.**; Stalles de Troisième Galerie, **1 fr. 50.**

Le Bureau de Location sera ouvert, au **THÉÂTRE DE LA RÉPUBLIQUE, rue de Malte, 50,** tous les jours, à partir de Mercredi, de 1 heure à 5 heures, et le jour du Concert, de 10 heures à midi.
S'adresser, pour les abonnements, au Secrétaire de l'**ASSOCIATION DES CONCERTS LAMOUREUX, 2, rue Moncey.**

On trouve des Billets : chez MM. DURAND et FILS, 4, place de la Madeleine; DUROILLY, 11 bis, boulevard Haussmann; L. GRUS, place Saint-Augustin; HAMELLE, 22, boulevard Malesherbes; NOEL, 22, passage des Panoramas; QUINZARD, 24, rue des Capucines; ROSENBERG, 51, boulevard Haussmann; ALLETON, 13, rue Racine.

12-99 10. — Paris, Typ. MORRIS Père et Fils, rue Amelot, 64

Program of Casals performance at the Théâtre de la République, Paris, with the Lamoureux Orchestra, December 17, 1899

On my return to Paris, there occurred an event which was to be a turning point in my career. The Count de Morphy had given me a letter of introduction to the celebrated French conductor, Charles Lamoureux, and I went to see him at his office. When I was ushered in, Lamoureux was seated at a writing table, bent over some papers. He was one of the most outstanding exponents of Wagner's music; he had conducted at the Bayreuth Festival and introduced *Lohengrin* and others of the great composer's works into France. Now he was preparing to give the first performance of *Tristan and Isolde* in Paris, and he was annotating the score. He was completely engrossed in his work. He didn't raise his head or give any indication he knew someone else was in the room. After standing there several minutes in silence, I began to feel embarrassed. Finally I said, "I am sorry, sir, to intrude upon your work. I only wish to give you a letter from the Count de Morphy." Lamoureux jerked his head toward me—he had a physical disability which made it painful for him to move his body or his legs. I noticed how pale he was—this great artist was suddenly to die before the end of the year—but his glance was a piercing one. He held out his hand without a word. I gave him the count's letter. He read it and said abruptly, "Come tomorrow morning, young man, and bring your cello with you."

The following morning I appeared again at Lamoureux's office. Seated at the piano was a young man, who I assumed was to be my accompanist. But, as on the previous day, Lamoureux was absorbed in his work and said nothing to me when I came in. So again I stood and waited. After a while he muttered something under his breath about people always disturbing him when he was trying to concentrate. "I certainly don't want to disturb you, sir," I said. "I shall leave right away."

He looked up from under his bushy eyebrows. "Young man," he said, "I like you. Play for me." With that, he went back to work on the score on his writing table.

I tuned up my cello. The accompanist and I started the Lalo concerto. I had barely played the opening notes when Lamoureux put down his pen. He listened intently for several seconds. Then, to my astonishment, he began to turn laboriously in his chair and drew himself painfully to his feet. He remained standing, facing us and leaning slightly forward, until the movement of the concerto was finished. Then he limped toward me and put his arms about me. There were tears in his eyes. He said, "My dear boy, you are one of the elect. You will play in my first concert next month."

I did not realize it at the time, but with those words of Lamoureux's the path was opened to whatever success has come to me through my music.

That October I made my Paris debut as a soloist at the Château d'Eau with the Lamoureux Orchestra—I played the Lalo concerto—and the following month I played again with him. The concerts were more successful than I could have dared hope for in my fondest dreams.

But my gratification was clouded. I could not share it with the man who had done so much to make it possible. Only a few weeks before, the Count de Morphy had died in Switzerland. He had been forced to leave Madrid because of certain difficulties at the court. I later learned that this noble person who had so enriched Spanish culture had died in virtual poverty. His death filled me with grief.

A chapter in my life had closed.

vi

Dawn of an Era

I was twenty-three years old at the turn of the century. It was a time of brave expectations. Many believed that a new epoch was at hand—that the dawn of the twentieth century would prove to be a turning point in the affairs of men. They cited recent scientific advances and predicted a future of great social progress. The era, they said, was approaching when poverty and hunger would at last disappear. In the way people make fervent resolutions at the start of a new year, the world seemed to be resolving at the start of a new century to undergo a change for the better. Who then foresaw that the coming decades would bring the unimaginable horrors of two world wars, concentration camps, and atomic bombs?

For me the future was full of promise. Almost overnight, following my concerts with Lamoureux, wide recognition came to me. I was besieged with requests to play at concerts and recitals. Suddenly all doors were open to me. It was heady wine for a young man at the start of his career. But I realized what circumstances had made all this possible for me. I had worked hard, it is true, but I had been greatly fortunate. Besides having been granted a certain talent by Nature, I had been blessed with a unique mother and father, with the friendship of a woman like Queen María Cristina, with teachers like the Count de Morphy, Monasterio, Bretón and García. Whatever I was, each of them was a part of me, and without any one of them I would have been that much less. This was true not only then; it is true also now. That is why gratitude and the knowledge of my debt have never left me.

Paris proved to be everything that François Gevaert had said it would be for me. It was *la belle epoch* when Paris was truly the cultural center of the world. The city was a mecca of creativity, the home and workshop of a galaxy of men of arts and letters. And in this city, with its teeming streets, its café terraces and chestnut vendors, its houses mellowed with the patina of centuries—here, where only a few short years ago my mother and I had faced such distress, I now found an exhilarating atmosphere for my work, new interests, and the companionship of brilliant men and women. My music, of course, brought me in close touch with other members of my profession. My circle of friends soon included such figures of the musical world as the violinists Eugène Ysaÿe and Jacques Thibaud, the pianists Harold Bauer and Alfred Cortot, the composers d'Indy, Enesco, Ravel, Arnold Schoenberg and Saint-Saëns. But my associations were by no means limited to musicians. I became acquainted with the artists Degas and Eugène Carrière, the statesmen Georges Clemenceau and Aristide Briand, the writer Romain Rolland, the philosopher Henri Bergson. They were fascinating men, and there was much to learn from them.

I found my talks with Bergson of special interest. We became very fond of one another, and I used to see him frequently. At first I was puzzled why this celebrated philosopher should want to spend time talking to a youth like me. I knew how intensely busy he was with his writings and his university lectures, and I felt that my knowledge

The score of a composition dedicated to Casals by Arnold Schoenberg

The score of a composition given to Casals by Camille Saint-Saëns was so limited—and he was a man of such vast erudition. But he assured me that he learned much from our conversations. One subject we talked a great deal about was that of intuition—it was, of course, a subject about which he had written a great deal. He was especially curious about the role of intuition in music. It has always been my viewpoint that intuition is the decisive element in both the composing and the performance of music. Of course technique and intelligence have vital functions—one must master the technique of an instrument in order to exact its full potentialities and one must apply one's intelligence in exploring every facet of the music—but, ultimately, the paramount role is that of intuition. For me the determining factor in creativity, in bringing a work to life, is that of musical instinct. . . .

I cannot say that everything I learned during those early days in Paris was pleasurable. The highest attainments of the human race are often matched by proofs of its follies and frailties. And while Paris shone with art and learning, there was also disquieting evidence of ignorance and social injustice. A shocking example was the notorious Dreyfus affair. I came to have an intimate knowledge of the case through my friendship with Colonel Georges Picquart, whom I met shortly after arriving in Paris. Colonel Picquart was an officer of a most unusual sort. Tall and distinguished-looking with a gray mustache, he was a very cultured man, gentle and charming—he was, among other things, a fine amateur pianist—and he had a consuming sense of justice. His motto was "Perfection in art, justice in life." It was this passion for justice that had involved him in the Dreyfus affair and resulted in his becoming one of its true heroes. He was too modest to think of his role in those terms, but it was so. I learned the inside story of the case through him.

At the time of my arrival, the affair was already a *cause*

célèbre. It was on everybody's lips. You would be at a musi-
cale, and before you knew it the music would be forgotten
and everyone would start talking about Captain Dreyfus.
Three or four years earlier, this Jewish officer had been
falsely accused of betraying military secrets to the Germans.
He was convicted with forged evidence by a court-martial
and sentenced to life imprisonment on the infamous Devils
Island. He would probably have died there if it had not been
for Colonel Picquart. The colonel, who was an official in the
French Ministry of War, had come upon some confidential
documents that convinced him Dreyfus was innocent. He
informed members of the French General Staff. They ordered him to drop the matter. Other officers might have
obeyed; not Colonel Picquart. He continued his investiga-
tion. The next thing he knew, he was ordered transferred to
a remote army post in Africa. But before leaving France he
gave the material he had uncovered to a prominent lawyer.
The matter was taken up in parliament. At first, few were
willing to come to Dreyfus' defense, and Colonel Picquart
himself was imprisoned on the charge of divulging secret
military information. But as more facts came to light, the
case became a national scandal. Émile Zola published his
famous open letter, *J'accuse!*, charging the government with
suppressing the truth. The protest reached such proportions
that the authorities were forced to bring Dreyfus back to
France for a second trial. New evidence, including the find-
ings of Colonel Picquart—he had by now been liberated—
clearly vindicated Dreyfus. But the army tried to save face.
They again found Dreyfus guilty—with extenuating circumstances, they said, and reduced his sentence to ten years
imprisonment! Soon after, the government pardoned Dreyfus. Still, his innocence was not officially admitted; and
Colonel Picquart and others went on fighting to clear his
name. Finally, several years later, Dreyfus was wholly ex-

onerated and reinstated in the army. And even then, Dreyfus' enemies were not satisfied with the suffering he had
endured. He was shot and wounded by an anti-Semitic
fanatic who tried to assassinate him!

All of this appalled and sickened me. I know that there
are those who believe artists should live in an ivory tower,
removed from the struggles and suffering of their fellow
men. That is a concept to which I have never been able to
subscribe. An affront to human dignity is an affront to me;
and to protest injustice is a matter of conscience. Are human
rights of less importance to an artist than to other men?
Does being an artist exempt one from his obligations as a
man? If anything, the artist has a particular responsibility,
because he has been granted special sensitivities and per-
ceptions, and because his voice may be heard when other
voices are not. Who, indeed, should be more concerned than
the artist with the defense of liberty and free inquiry, which
are essential to his very creativity?

For me, perhaps the most frightful aspect of the Dreyfus
affair was the fact that many people were against him because he was Jewish. And I found it almost unbelievable
that in Paris—with all its culture and its noble traditions of
the rights of man—that here, in this city which was called
la ville lumière, anti-Semitism could spread like a foul
plague. What words, indeed, are there to describe this disease, which would later infect a whole nation and rationalize
the massacre of millions of men, women and children on
the grounds that "Jewish blood" flowed in their veins?
One's mind staggers at the monstrosity!

The very idea of hating Jews is incomprehensible to me.
My own life has been so enriched by tender associations
with Jewish fellow artists and friends. What people on
earth have contributed more to human culture than the
Jewish people? Of course they make wonderful musicians.

The reason is that they have so much heart—yes, and head, too! When I am conducting and tell the orchestra members, "Play Jewish," they know what I mean. My friend Sasha Schneider sometimes says to me, "You know, Don Pablo, you are really Jewish." He will not listen to my claim that my parents were Catholic and I am a Catalan. He shakes his head good-naturedly and says, "No, you are wrong. You may have been born of Catholic parents in Catalonia, but actually you are Jewish. For one thing, you could not play as you do if you were not." I appreciate that compliment, but I tell Sasha that there are exceptions to every rule.

It was in the year 1901 that I made my first trip to the United States. I traveled with Emma Nevada and a talented young French pianist, Léon Moreau. We came for a tour of eighty concerts. Our advance manager on the tour was Raymond Duncan, the brother of that remarkable woman, Isadora Duncan.

I could not then anticipate how the thread of my life would be woven into the tapestry of this great land, and how more than half a century later I would find my home in this hemisphere. But the country had a profound effect upon me. I had heard much about America—particularly from Emma Nevada, whose homeland, after all, it was—but there are certain things that cannot be comprehended without being experienced. America was such a phenomenon for me. What striking differences there were between America and the European countries with which I was familiar! We visited dozens of towns and cities, and journeyed across the continent from the Atlantic to the Pacific; and even so, as the land unfolded before me, with its vast prairies, huge mountain ranges and awesome deserts, I knew I was catching only a glimpse of its immensity. Never before had I been so overwhelmed by Nature's grandeur and diversity; and never before had I been more conscious of the invincible spirit of man, who had penetrated these spaces and made them his home. You felt that man could accomplish anything and that everything for his happiness was possible here.

The New World ceased to be a mere phrase to me. Newness abounded on all sides. One sensed a nation still in the process of coming into being, like a great symphony in rehearsal.

Of course, the America of 1901 was not the America of today. There were large cities, yes, but there were also frontier towns. There were regions where the wilderness was still unconquered and places that made me feel as if I myself were a pioneer! And even the cities bore little resemblance to those of today. Then, you could still see the sky—smog and skyscrapers had not yet been invented. Only occasionally did you come upon a strange contraption that was called an automobile. And I must confess that when I now visit New York or Chicago, I sometimes feel nostalgic for those days when there were no taxis creeping along in traffic and a comfortable horse-drawn carriage would take you without delay wherever you wanted to go. . . .

At that time certain European intellectuals had a scornful attitude toward the United States. Americans, they said, were lacking in culture and artistic achievement. But one of the things that greatly impressed me during that first visit and on subsequent trips was the extensive concern with culture, and especially music, among Americans. I was struck by the emphasis on musical education in the schools, with their bands, orchestras and choral groups, and I was frequently amazed at the interest in music and the musical facilities—often crude, of course—in out-of-the-way places and little remote towns.

But most of all, I think, I was impressed by the feeling of

equality among the people. I was accustomed to the class distinctions of Europe, and, with my republican upbringing and beliefs, I had always felt them absurd and offensive. I had never recognized any distinction between men, or thought some deserved special privileges because of the accident of birth or the accumulation of wealth. And now I felt I was in a society where merit—whatever inequities had yet to be solved—was judged by character and capability.

For me, at the age of twenty-four, America was an emancipation. . . .

My colleague on that tour, Léon Moreau, was a bit of a daredevil, always ready for some new adventure. And I myself was full of curiosity. We had no desire to confine ourselves to hotel rooms and concert halls. We wanted to see everything we could of this strange, exciting land. No sooner had we arrived in a new town and unpacked our things than we'd be off exploring. We were frequently involved in bizarre experiences.

I remember that when we came to the little mining town of Wilkes-Barre in Pennsylvania, we decided we had to see a mine. It was late in the afternoon but that did not deter us. We made the necessary inquiries and hurried off. At the mine, we were taken down into the pit. It was a mysterious and fascinating place—so fascinating, in fact, that we forgot about everything else as we explored the tunnels and talked to the miners. All at once Moreau said, "What about the concert? What time is it?" It was almost time for the concert to start! There was not a moment to spare to return to the hotel and change our clothes. We rushed straight to the concert hall without even washing our hands and faces. When we arrived, we looked more like miners than musicians! But we cleaned up as best we could and went ahead with the performance.

The Wild West was still a reality in those days—when

I now watch cowboy programs on television, I'm reminded of some of the Western towns where we gave concerts on that tour. Great excitement would attend our arrival. There would be large streamers over the streets announcing the concert, and printed posters on the walls of buildings—sometimes next to a poster offering a reward for some wanted outlaw. The halls in which we played were often roughly built but they were always packed, and the concerts took place in a gay, boisterous atmosphere, with ushers parading through the aisles during the intermissions selling peanuts and candy. One day when Moreau and I were out for a stroll in one of those Western towns, we wandered into a saloon. We were soon involved in a poker game with several cowboys—they were sturdy-looking fellows with guns in their belts. My experience as a gambler was limited, but I was lucky enough—or perhaps I should say unlucky enough—to start winning consistently. As the silver coins piled up in front of me, I noticed that the expressions on the faces of the other cardplayers were growing grim. A tense mood settled over the game. I looked at the revolvers of my opponents, and the thought occurred to me that our concert tour might come to an abrupt and unforeseen conclusion! Everyone was drinking whiskey. One of the cowboys offered me a glass. I declined as politely as possible, saying I didn't drink while gambling—I didn't add that I rarely drank while not gambling. The cowboy retorted, "Here we drink *and* gamble." Finally the cards changed, and I was fortunate enough to start losing. The climate suddenly improved. Everyone began to smile. When the time came for Moreau and me to leave the saloon, we all embraced like old friends.

On another occasion a fellow passenger on a train asked me if I had ever gone out into an American desert. When I said I hadn't, he told me, "You really must. It will be an experience you'll never forget." And he was right. The op-

portunity came when we stopped for an engagement at a
small desert town in Texas. Even Moreau had some misgivings about our walking off into the vast wasteland
surrounding the town, but I was adamant. The desert was
truly amazing—once in it, you felt you were on another
planet. After a while Moreau said, "Don't you think we've
walked far enough? Let's go back." But just then I saw, far
off in the distance, what appeared to be some sort of house.
"You wait here," I told Moreau. "I want to go and see what
that building is. Then I'll come back." He wouldn't let me
go alone; so we walked on together for another half hour
or so until we reached the building. It was a weatherbeaten
shack, and it seemed at first to be deserted. However, inside
we found a man and a woman. We were hot and tired, and
they gave us something to drink. The man was dressed like
a cowboy, but I noticed something strange about his accent.

"You are not of this country," I said to him.

He replied, "No, I come from across the water."

"And from where?"

"Oh, it's a country you never heard of."

"And what is the name of that country?" I inquired.

"Its name," he said, "is Catalonia."

So there we were, two fellow Catalans in the middle of
the American desert!

It is a fact that you will find Catalans everywhere.

Indeed, long before that curious rendezvous in the Texas
desert, other travelers from Catalonia had left their mark
on America. In the city of Barcelona, overlooking the harbor, there is a pillar on the top of which stands a monument
of Christopher Columbus with his hand stretched toward
the west. It was to Barcelona that Columbus returned to
first report his discovery of the New World to Fernando
and Isabel; and the only communications of Columbus that
remain are written not in Italian but in Catalan—they bear

the signature "Colom," which means "pigeon" in the Catalan tongue. When I came to California for the first time, I
was also aware that the first European to explore much of
this region was the Franciscan missionary, Fra Junípero Serra, who founded the San Francisco mission in the year of the
American Revolution. Fra Serra was born on the Catalan
island of Majorca. . . .

In San Francisco I had an experience which not only
brought my first American tour to a sudden end but almost
ended my career as a cellist. I was enchanted by the city and
by the surrounding countryside. And when several young,
newly made friends invited me to join them on an expedi-
tion across the Bay to climb Mount Tamalpais, I was delighted. I have always loved mountain climbing. We crossed
on a ferryboat which was, I think, the most ornate vessel I'd
ever seen—a veritable floating castle.

It was when we were making our descent on Mount Tamalpais that the accident occurred. Suddenly one of my
companions shouted, "Watch out, Pablo!" I looked up and
saw a boulder hurtling down the mountainside directly
toward me. I jerked my head aside and was lucky not to be
killed. As it was, the boulder hit and smashed my left hand
—my fingering hand. My friends were aghast. But when I
looked at my mangled bloody fingers, I had a strangely
different reaction. My first thought was "Thank God, I'll
never have to play the cello again!" No doubt, a psycho-
analyst would give some profound explanation. But the
fact is that dedication to one's art does involve a sort of en-
slavement, and then too, of course, I have always felt such
dreadful anxiety before performances.

I remained in San Francisco while Emma Nevada and
Moreau continued the tour. The doctors predicted I'd never
regain the full use of my hand. But doctors sometimes make
mistakes. With constant treatments and exercise, my hand

healed completely, after four months, and I started practicing again. I fell in love with San Francisco—who does not? —and I formed associations that would last throughout the years. I stayed at the home of Michael Stein, the president of the city's cable car company. He was a highly cultured man, a patron of the arts, wonderfully hospitable. His house was full of paintings, books and magazines in various languages—everyone seemed to be always reading and making voluminous notes—and the conversation constantly turned to art. He had a younger sister who was studying medicine, a sturdy young woman in her twenties with a strong handsome face. She had a brilliant mind and a vivid way of expressing herself. Her name was Gertrude. Of course Gertrude Stein was not then world-renowned.

Once when I was sitting with my injured hand in a plaster cast, Gertrude said, "You look like El Greco's *Gentleman With a Hand on His Chest.*"

I laughed and told her, "Well, even if I can't play, my fingers are at least resting on the true instrument of all art and music."

In later years I used to see Gertrude Stein and another brother of hers, Leo, when they moved to Paris, where she became a legendary figure in the world of art and letters and he became an eminent art critic. Whenever I visited Gertrude's little studio flat near the Luxembourg Gardens, I would find her reading and Leo drawing. The walls of the flat were crowded with paintings. "These pictures," she would tell me, "are by young painters that nobody wants to pay any attention to." They were works by Matisse, Picasso and others. I had met Picasso in the late 1890's when he was still an art student in Barcelona, and even then I had a great admiration for his work, but somehow our paths never crossed in Paris. . . .

One precious friendship I formed during my first visit to

San Francisco was with a young woman named Theresa Hermann, whose father was a rabbi. She played the piano and her sister was a violinist. She was one of the party on that memorable outing to Mount Tamalpais. Our friendship was to last almost seven decades. Whenever I went to California, I would see her, and after the Casals Festival was inaugurated in Puerto Rico in the 1950's, she came to attend the performances. I was greatly saddened by her recent death. She was one of the last of my friends from those early days. Yes, many memories remain but, alas, few friends. . . .

In 1904 I toured the United States for the second time. I made my first appearance with the Metropolitan Orchestra in New York City, playing the Saint-Saëns concerto. That same season I played as a cello soloist in the first New York performance of Richard Strauss's symphonic poem, *Don Quixote*, with the great composer himself conducting. The performance was very well received, but there were some promotional people who thought I should cut a more dramatic figure on the concert stage. Histrionics were fashionable then, and musical talent was sometimes judged by the length of one's hair. My own hair has never been excessive —in fact, I had already started to grow bald—and my manager told me I could command considerably higher fees for my performances in America if only I'd wear a wig while playing. . . .

I had an unfortunate experience with my manager on that tour. Throughout my career I have tried to have as little to do with money as possible. Of course money is an unfortunate necessity of existence, and I'm aware it is sometimes put to altruistic uses. But I find something distasteful about money and dislike handling it. During my concert tours my managers always settled all financial matters. They would collect my fees and deposit them to my account. My manager did this during my second trip to the United States. But on that occasion I discovered that he was getting a considerably larger sum from each of the concerts than he'd told me I was being paid. I was very angry—not because of the money but because of the man's dishonesty.

When I returned to New York City at the end of the tour, I telephoned my manager and asked him to come to my hotel. He suggested we meet at his office, but I said no, that he should come to me. I went into the lobby and put a small table and a couple of chairs near the revolving doors that served as the entrance to the hotel. I waited for him there. When he came, I asked him to sit down with me at the table.

He said, "How was the tour?"

I said, "Everything was fine—except for one thing."

"And what was that?" he asked.

"I had a thief for a manager," I said.

He went white, absolutely white, and his eyes got very big. "What are you talking about!" he said.

"No," I told him, "there is no sense in your lying. I know exactly how much you took from each of my concerts."

He stood up, stammering.

Then—as I had planned—I seized him and thrust him into the revolving doors. I spun the doors around and around as fast as I could. He went whirling about inside. I pushed the doors so hard that they broke. He staggered out and ran down the street.

Of course I had to pay for the doors. I had expected that. I never got any of the money he had taken, but I really didn't mind that either. I think I taught him a lesson.

More than half a century later, when I went to Washington to play for President Kennedy, some newspapers reported that this was my first appearance at the White

House. Actually, I had previously played there for President Roosevelt—not Franklin Delano Roosevelt but Theodore Roosevelt. That was during my visit to America in 1904.

The performance took place at a reception given by the President. He had an infectious joviality. He put his arm around my shoulders after the concert and led me around among the guests, introducing me to everyone and talking all the time. I felt that in a sense he personified the American nation, with all his energy, strength and confidence. It was not hard to picture him galloping on a horse or hunting big game, as he was so fond of doing.

On the occasion of my subsequent visit to the White House in 1961, I was introduced to a handsome white-haired lady who told me that she had been present as a young woman when I first played there. Her name was Mrs. Nicholas Longworth, and she was, of course, Theodore Roosevelt's daughter.

vii

Family of Man

Within a few years after I moved to Paris, I was to become familiar with a score of foreign lands. In my heart Catalonia remained my home, but I came to feel at home in St. Petersburg and São Paulo, Philadelphia and Budapest, London, Venice, Stockholm, Buenos Aires. Traveling then was not of course what it is today. To fly over the Atlantic now takes a few hours; my crossing with Emma Nevada and Léon Moreau took eighteen days. I traveled tens of thousands of miles. The years became a kaleidoscope of new places, new acquaintances, new impressions.

I lost track of the number of concerts I gave. I do know it was often around two hundred and fifty a year. Sometimes when I was traveling in countries where cities were close together, I'd give over thirty concerts a month—on Sundays I would often have one concert in the afternoon and another in the evening. It was a demanding schedule. I never missed an engagement. I had a strong constitution, but even so I sometimes felt exhausted. Once, in Berlin, I fainted in the middle of a performance, but after a short rest I finished the concert.

I must say it was not an ideal form of existence. I have never liked packing and unpacking. Even for a young man, full of energy and curiosity, the excitement of travel wears off; and to spend a night here, a weekend there, and to hurry on—to have to rush to catch trains after concerts when your clothing is still drenched with perspiration, and to travel all night and have a rehearsal the following morning —becomes fatiguing and frustrating. Then too there was the sadness of leaving newfound friends. Regardless of how successful my concert tours were, I was always glad when they were over and I returned to Paris. I was happiest of all when summer came—then I could visit Catalonia and see my mother and father.

However, though I often longed for home, I cannot say I was lonely. I had my constant companions—Bach, Beethoven, Brahms, Mozart. And on many concert tours I traveled with fellow musicians, dear friends, like Harold Bauer, Alfred Cortot, Jacques Thibaud and Fritz Kreisler. And no matter in what country I was or where I performed—whether it was in the Hall of Nobles in Moscow or a high-school auditorium in Maryland, I never felt I was a stranger in a foreign land. I was often grateful that the Count de Morphy had insisted on my learning several foreign languages—I became quite fluent in seven—but it was essentially through music that I communicated with people wherever I went. If their native tongue was different from mine, the language of our hearts was the same. You could cross borders and sleep in strange towns, but always find this common comradeship of spirit.

To see people gathered in a concert hall came to have a symbolic significance for me. When I looked into their faces, and when we shared the beauty of music, I knew that we were brothers and sisters, all members of the same family. Despite the dreadful conflicts of the intervening years and all the false barriers between nations, that knowledge has never left me. It will remain with me until the end. I long for the day when the peoples of the world will sit together,

Casals in an artist's studio in Holland in 1907

bound by happiness and love of beauty, as in one great concert hall!

It was shortly after my debut with Lamoureux that I came to know Harold Bauer. He was then twenty-six and already widely known as a pianist. Actually, he had started his career as a violinist. He was a handsome young man with sparkling eyes and bushy red hair; once, when he was still a youngster in England, Paderewski had jokingly told him, "You would make a fine pianist; you have such beautiful hair." When Bauer settled in Paris a few years later, he did become a pianist. And what a superb one! He was an especially wonderful interpreter of Brahms, Schumann and Chopin. We took an immediate liking to one another when we met, and Bauer suggested we give some joint concerts. We arranged a number in Spain and Holland. That was in 1900. It was the beginning of a long and joyful association. In the ensuing years I would give more concerts with Bauer than with any other performer. We complemented one another wonderfully well. There was an instinctive communion between us, and we shared the same views about music. From the beginning it was as if we had been playing together for years.

Bauer was a delightful companion—a brilliant man, sensitive, perceptive, with a keen sense of humor and a remarkable knack for mimicry. He was an omnivorous reader—he always traveled with a dozen or so books—and when we were on a boat he would spend hours rummaging through the ship's library, making copious notes and reading late into the night. Like me, he was fond of athletics, and quite often we would wrestle in our cabin. He was a good deal larger than I was, but I was very strong in those days and usually managed to get him down. Sometimes we made so much noise that the steward would come to our cabin in alarm. Bauer would tell them, "What's the matter? It's nothing. We're just doing our daily exercises."

Bauer, however, had one most vexing problem; he suffered greatly from seasickness. He tried every imaginable remedy—at one time, in fact, he even wore some sort of device which was supposed to hold his stomach muscles in such a position as to prevent his becoming ill. But nothing worked. It was a miserable affliction.

One of our early trips took us to Brazil in 1903. It was my first trip to South America. We performed in Rio de Janeiro and a number of other cities. The tour was arranged by a most remarkable man who had previously organized a concert for me in Oporto, Portugal. His name was Moreira de Sa, and he was one of those rare individuals who can do almost anything—and do it well. Besides being a successful businessman, he was an eminent scholar, a brilliant mathematician, an author of school textbooks, a philosopher, an artist. In addition to everything else, he was a fine musician—he played the violin exceedingly well. He traveled with Bauer and me to Brazil and performed with us on a number of occasions. At the end of the tour, shortly before we were due to sail back to Europe, Moreira de Sa came to Bauer and me and told us very apologetically that he couldn't return with us. An unexpected development, he said, made it imperative for him to remain in Rio for several more weeks. Then, with great excitement, he told us what it was. He had just met a man who was an expert in the technique of Japanese lacquer, an art, he said, which he himself had always longed to learn; and the man had offered to teach it to him. And so Moreira de Sa stayed on in Brazil!

Traveling with Bauer was never dull, and we frequently shared amusing experiences. One occurred during that first visit of ours to Brazil in the city of São Paolo. We were rehearsing at our hotel before the performance and didn't realize how late it was until it was almost time for the concert to begin. We rushed into our evening clothes. I was pulling on my trousers when one of my feet got stuck. I pushed hard in exasperation—and, all at once, my foot went right through the trouser leg! I was horrified. The damage looked beyond repair—the whole bottom portion was ripped open. What was I to do? Even Bauer for once had nothing witty to say. We summoned a maid and showed her the torn trousers. She scurried off and returned with needle and thread. While we counted the seconds, she sewed up the rip as best she could. The workmanship might have been neater, but I could not have been more grateful—at least, I had a pair of trousers to wear during the concert.

I was reminded of that incident only recently when a friend sent me a newspaper clipping from San Francisco. A young woman, apparently influenced by the topless fad, was on trial for playing the cello in a state of dishabille. The judge told her that he questioned the artistic merits of a topless performance on the cello. He said, "I doubt if Pablo Casals would have been a better cellist if he had played without trousers." Since I have never given a concert in that condition, I cannot challenge the judge's opinion. That night in São Paolo almost seventy years ago was the closest I have ever come to performing without trousers—though sometimes, I must admit, when it is warm here in Puerto Rico, I do wear shorts while practicing.

In 1905, following my return from my second tour of the United States, I began my musical collaboration with the Swiss-born pianist, Alfred Cortot, and the French violinist, Jacques Thibaud. It was an association that would continue over a period of three decades. When we started playing together as a trio, I was twenty-eight, Cortot twenty-seven, and Thibaud twenty-four—and our combined ages were considerably less than mine is today!

I have mentioned I would far rather play chamber music than solos, and our trio offered me the ideal opportunity. We understood each other perfectly in our music, and we formed a marvelously gratifying team—not only as an ensemble but as friends. We began the custom of devoting one month each year to traveling together to give chamber-music concerts, and our trio soon became widely known.

We also joined in making some of the earliest recordings of classical music on the gramophone—I had already made some on a cylinder around 1903. Certain of these recordings of ours, like the one of the Schubert Trio in B Flat, which was to remain in demand for many years, helped dispel the early prejudice among musicians against the gramophone. Of course the instrument was then in its infancy, and it left much to be desired. As a matter of fact, even to this day I find phonograph recordings far from fully satisfying.

Cortot and Thibaud were superlative artists. Cortot was unquestionably one of the great pianists of our time—he had boundless *élan* and astonishing power. He was also a brilliant musical scholar, whose writings on piano technique and musical appreciation gained international recognition. He interpreted Beethoven magnificently, and he had a consuming admiration for Wagner. For a time, when still in his twenties, he had been an assistant conductor at Bayreuth, and at the age of twenty-four he conducted the first Paris performance of *Götterdämmerung.* Perhaps his most treasured possession was a portrait of Wagner by Renoir. He was an indefatigable, highly disciplined worker, both as a musician and as a scholar, and he was very ambitious for his career. I think it was perhaps this ambition which led to the sorrowful events that later overtook him.

Thibaud had been a protégé of the famous French conductor, Édouard Colonne—Colonne had discovered him when he was playing as a youth in the Café Rouge in Paris and had launched him on his concert career. Like Cortot, he was a consummate instrumentalist—he played the violin with an incomparable elegance. But in many ways he was Cortot's opposite. He hated work and rarely practiced. He had, you might say, no sense of responsibility—he often behaved like a child, a naughty child. But he was wonderfully witty and gay. When the three of us were on tour, he kept us constantly entertained. He loved practical jokes, and he had a really remarkable inventiveness for them.

Once, I remember, when we had to catch a train quite early in the morning and were getting ready to leave our hotel, Thibaud suddenly went to a room near ours and knocked loudly on the door. A man's sleepy voice asked, "Who is there?"

Thibaud said, "The barber, sir."

"The barber? There's some mistake. I don't want a barber."

Thibaud said, "I beg your pardon, sir."

A few minutes later, he knocked on the door again.

"Yes?"

"It's the barber, sir."

"I already told you I don't want a barber!"

Then Thibaud went downstairs to the barber and told him the guest in that room wanted his services immediately —the man, said Thibaud, was very annoyed because he'd left word the night before that he wanted a barber the first thing in the morning. The barber hurried off. One can imagine the reception he got!

Sometimes our impresario, Boquel, traveled with us, and Thibaud was constantly playing jokes on him. Boquel was very fastidious—he even wore gloves when playing cards. On one occasion he went out of the room during a card game and left his gloves on the table. When he put them on after coming back, he found his fingers projecting from their ends. In his absence Thibaud had cut off the finger tips! Another time, when Boquel started to brush his hair

just before one of our concerts, he found to his horror that
his brush was coated with butter—it was, of course, Thibaud's doing. Naturally, Boquel became rather piqued by
this sort of thing.

Around the time that I began giving concerts with Cortot
and Thibaud, I met another musician—a very much younger one—who is today my oldest friend and associate. I
speak of that marvelous pianist, Mieczyslaw Horszowski.
He was a boy when we met. I have known him for more
than sixty years, and we have now been playing together
for half a century! He is the one remaining friend with
whom I can reminisce about associates and experiences that
date back to my youth.

Horszowski was born in Poland in the early 1890's and
was a child prodigy—he made a sensational debut at the
age of nine. He came to Spain with his mother in 1905 on
one of his earliest concert tours and played in Barcelona. I
was in Paris at the time, but my brother Enrique heard him
play and was greatly excited. Enrique arranged for Mme.
Horszowski and her son to meet my mother. Our two
mothers got on wonderfully well—they had much in common and loved to be together. My mother wrote me about
all of this. A few months later, I met Horszowski in Italy.

He was brought to see me at the house of a friend after
one of my concerts. I can vividly remember the occasion.
He was very small—diminutive—and very shy, and he was
dressed in a sailor suit with short trousers and a large white
collar trimmed with lace. He looked about ten years old,
though he tells me he was thirteen; and this must be right,
because he is always extremely precise and meticulous. He
played for me, and I was deeply impressed. I knew he had a
great talent.

Two or three years later he came to see me in Paris, and
I worked with him, especially on Bach. After the First

World War, we were to give many chamber-music concerts together in Italy, England, Switzerland and other countries. Later he played for my orchestra in Barcelona and at my music festivals in Prades and Puerto Rico. To this day we play together.

A remarkable thing about Horszowski is that in many ways he seems to have hardly changed since we first met. Despite his immense talent as a musician, he is still very shy and extraordinarily modest and retiring. And still very small—in fact, smaller than I am! I've really never known anyone who has remained so unchanged over the years. When I look at him now, I see him as a small boy—though I must say he has given up one infatuation he used to have. As a young man, before the Great War, he had a passion for sports cars, racing cars; and each summer he used to take one of those little cars with two seats and drive it at a great pace from Paris to the French Riviera and on into Italy. Of course that sort of thing was much more difficult in those days than today. The roads, he has told me, were terrible— they were very dusty and full of nails, which often got into his tires. . . .

In 1905 I made my Russian debut. The time at which I arrived was hardly a propitious one for a concert tour. Though I did not know it when I left Paris for an engagement in Moscow, the Revolution of 1905 had already begun.

Shortly after we crossed the Russian frontier, our train was stopped at Vilna and everyone was told to get off. There was bedlam at the railroad station. Baggage was piled high, and scores of people were milling about, shouting and gesticulating. I could understand little of what was being said, because most of the people were, of course, speaking Russian. In the waiting room I was approached by a man wearing a uniform, who introduced himself to me. He was a high railway official and a general in the Russian army, and he seemed to know a great deal about my work. All traffic to Moscow, he said, had been halted by a railroad strike. However, a special train was about to depart for St. Petersburg. Did I wish to accompany him on it? I thought of the return trip of more than a thousand miles to Paris and gratefully accepted his offer. As we traveled north across the snowy Russian countryside, I wondered what lay in store for me.

As soon as we reached St. Petersburg, I went to see the conductor Alexander Siloti. I had corresponded with him and knew his reputation. As a young man he had been a brilliant pianist—he had studied for a time with Tchaikovsky and then with Liszt, who exercised a great influence upon him—and later he had emerged as one of the foremost conductors in Russia. Now he was directing an orchestra in St. Petersburg. Siloti received me most cordially. I was astonished at his resemblance to Liszt; he could have been Liszt's twin brother, he even had a wart on his face like Liszt. He insisted that I stay with him—he had a lovely house near the River Neva with a magnificent music library. When I told him about being unable to get to Moscow, he said he too faced a problem because of the railroad strike— a soloist he had engaged couldn't reach St. Petersburg. He asked me if I would play in the soloist's place. I readily agreed. The concert was held in a highly dramatic atmosphere. There was no electricity because of a general strike in the city, and the hall was lit by candlelight. The audience was wonderfully responsive.

I remained in St. Petersburg for two or three weeks and gave a series of concerts with Siloti. A tense and ominous mood hung over the city. The nights were punctuated with gunfire. One had the feeling that anything might happen at any moment. There were riots across the River Neva, and I told Siloti I wanted to go and see what was happening. He said, "Don't be foolish. Do you want to get shot?" But finally, one night after a concert, he gave in to me. We took a carriage across one of the bridges. On the other side, we heard shots nearby. Suddenly a man waving a flag came rushing around a corner. He shouted wildly in Russian as he passed our carriage. I asked what he was shouting. Siloti told me, "He's shouting, 'Long live the Republic of the Czars!'"

Such was the state of mind at the time! The Russians desperately wanted an end to the autocracy under which they had suffered for so long, but many had been so indoctrinated that they could not conceive of a republic without a czar at the head of it!

On a subsequent trip to Russia, I myself experienced something of the repressive measures of the period following the suppression of the Revolution of 1905. I was challenged at the border by several Czarist officials—big hulking men in uniform—who acted as if I were some sort of dangerous subversive. I couldn't imagine what they suspected. They barked at me in Russian, and when I replied in German that I couldn't understand them, they paid no attention. After rummaging through my baggage, they searched me from head to foot—they even forced me to undress! I was furious. When I reached St. Petersburg, I told Siloti what had happened. He was, if anything, more outraged than I was. He reported the affair to the government authorities, and I received an official apology. The episode, I was told, was all an unfortunate mistake. The explanation did little to assuage my feelings.

There was ample evidence of the heavy hand of the rulers. On all sides one felt apprehension, suspicion, fear. Everyone was spied on. Doormen and janitors had to report to the Czarist police what happened in the houses where they worked. The secret police themselves were everywhere. The great composer Rimski-Korsakov was dismissed for a time from his professorship at the St. Petersburg Conserva-

tory of Music for publishing a protest against secret police
surveillance of the students. People were afraid to say anything against the government. You often felt as if you were
in a prison.

On my various trips to Russia, besides playing in St.
Petersburg, I gave concerts in Moscow, Riga, Kiev and other
cities. And wherever I went, I was struck by the glaring con-
trasts—on the one hand, the dreadful poverty among the
working people, and, on the other, the flagrantly ostenta-
tious wealth of the aristocrats. I was convinced it was only
a matter of time before the people revolted again against
these unbearable conditions. When the storm finally burst
in 1917, I felt that the inevitable had happened. At the same
time, I must say that I have been appalled by the injustices
and repressions that have followed that Revolution. I am
aware that in every revolution certain excesses seem inevitable—I myself have witnessed something of the violent ex-
tremes to which people in rebellion will go. But I cannot
condone the actions of those who, in the name of social
change, persecute innocent people, many of whom have
themselves worked for the betterment of society. No ends
and no achievements can justify such means.

It was my good fortune to become acquainted with a
number of the noted Russian composers—Rimski-Korsakov, Scriabin, César Cui, Glazunov, and others. In Moscow
I frequently played under the direction of Rachmaninoff.
Immensely gifted men! When one realizes the phenomenal
rapidity with which classical music had flowered in Russia,
their works seem all the more remarkable. And with what
kindness they treated me!

I remember in particular one experience with Rimski-
Korsakov. It happened in St. Petersburg when Siloti took
me to a performance of one of Rimski-Korsakov's operas at
the Maryinsky Theater. During the intermission after the

first act, Glazunov—he had been a pupil of Rimski-Korsakov—came to the box where Siloti and I were seated. He told me, "I've just been talking with Nikolai Andreevich, and he's nervous because you're here. He's afraid you won't like the music." Imagine the modesty of the man! He was then in his sixties and at the height of his career, and I was not yet thirty. I felt embarrassed to reply. But I asked Glazunov to please let Rimski-Korsakov know how greatly I was enjoying the opera. After the performance I met with Rimski-Korsakov, and I told him how much I loved his music. And he evidenced such appreciation!

It always struck me as curious that this great Russian composer was also a high officer in the Russian navy. However, I never saw him in his uniform. The composer who often did wear his uniform was César Cui, and—with his full white beard and piercing eyes—he cut a very distinguished figure in it. He was a general in the czar's army, and I was told he was a leading authority on artillery and things of that sort. His father had been a French officer who stayed behind during Napoleon's retreat from Moscow in 1812. César Cui was, I think you could say, one of the few blessings that Napoleon brought to Russia.

Of the Russian composers I met, Alexander Scriabin unquestionably made the most dramatic impression on me. He was a truly astonishing person. He was a real innovator and, in fact, an inventor, a pioneer who explored ideas not only in music but in philosophy. He was always experimenting with harmonics and orchestration. Like Rimski-Korsakov and César Cui, interestingly enough, he had started his career in the military service. Then he had turned to music and become widely known as a pianist before he became a composer. He was still in his thirties when we met—a handsome man with a waxed mustache and a small beard. He discussed many of his ideas with me. It was his contention that music as we knew it was in many ways crude and rudimentary, and that our musical scale was far too limited and superficial. He was intensely interested in a relationship between music and color, and he believed, in fact, that scales, corresponding to musical scales, should be developed for other senses, for color, taste and smell. He felt that all possibilities of aesthetic sensations should be investigated. He asserted that someone listening to music was inevitably affected by the surroundings in which the music was played—that the effects of music heard in darkness were quite different from those of music heard in light, and that one's sensations responded to variations in color just as to changes in temperature. He invited me to his house in Moscow and showed me an apparatus he had developed for reproducing sound in color. I think I must have been one of the first to see it. It was really remarkable and produced marvelous effects. He was composing a new orchestral work, *Prometheus,* for which he was writing a part for a keyboard of lights, so that various colors could play on a screen while the work was performed. It was the first time that anything like this had been done. And to think that this amazing genius was only forty-three when he died a few years after we met! At the time of his death, he was composing a monumental work, which involved some two thousand participants and combined musical effects with those of dance, song, speech, color and even perfume!

In the years following my settling in Paris, I performed in every European capital—with one exception. That exception was, incongruously, the city for which I felt the greatest musical affinity—Vienna. Much as I longed to play there, I could not muster the courage. For almost a decade I declined one invitation after another and kept away, like a man who fears to come too close to the thing he loves the most. I was drawn to that city of legendary charm as by a magnet, but I was haunted by the living ghosts that dwelt there. For me, Vienna was the very Temple of Music, which still echoed with the works of Mozart, Beethoven, Brahms, Schubert, Haydn. Their spirits had inhabited me since my childhood; yet now I hesitated to enter their home. For this was where they had lived and loved, labored, suffered and died. Finally, and with great trepidation, I accepted an engagement to play in Vienna. I have never known such apprehension before a concert. I wandered through the streets with my heart pounding—I had the feeling that at any moment I might come face to face with Mozart or Schubert, that suddenly Beethoven would stand before me, looking at me silently and with immeasurable sadness, as over the years I had seen him in my dreams. The concert was held at the Musikfreunde hall. Not a seat was vacant. The work I had selected to play was Emanuel Moór's Concerto in C-Sharp Minor. I drew my bow across the strings for the first notes and suddenly, with panic, I felt it slipping from my fingers. I tried desperately to regain control of it but my movement was too abrupt. The bow shot from my grasp, and as I watched in helpless horror, it flew over the heads of the first rows of the audience! There was not a sound in the hall. Someone retrieved the bow. It was handed with tender care from person to person—still in utter silence; and as I followed its slow passage toward me with fascination, a strange thing happened. My nervousness completely vanished. When the bow reached me, I immediately began the concerto again and this time with absolute confidence. I think I have never played better than I did that night.

From then on, I visited Vienna every year.

As I have already related, my first visit to the city of Brussels at the age of nineteen was not a happy one and I gladly left after two days. On a later occasion, when my reputation as a cellist was already established, I had another experience which was also disturbing, though it ended more fortunately.

This experience occurred at the rehearsal for a concert at which I was to perform with a symphony orchestra. There was a custom which I regarded as long outdated and an imposition on musicians. The final rehearsal before a concert would be attended by an audience which was charged admission—but the artists themselves were paid only for their performance at the actual concert. On this occasion, I decided that the time had come to do something about this custom. So during the final rehearsal, which took place in a full auditorium, I acted as I would at any other rehearsal. I stopped whenever I felt the need for any correction in the concerto I was playing and discussed the point in detail with the conductor. Before long the audience began getting restless. When the concerto was finished, the director of the conservatory asked me to proceed with the Bach suite which was scheduled for the second part of the program. I told him, "Oh, that's not necessary. I've already practiced that enough. I don't need to rehearse it now." He said, "But you must play it. Everyone is expecting you to." I said I was very sorry but I had no intention of doing so. In the meantime quite a commotion arose in the hall and some of the audience began calling out and asking when the music was going to continue. Finally the director said, "I must beseech you, Monsieur Casals—please play the Bach suite. Consider yourself engaged for two concert performances. I shall see to it that you are paid for both." I said all right and went ahead. When the actual concert was over, I received two fees, but I told the director I would keep only one. The other, I insisted, was to go to the orchestra's fund. After that, the practice of having paying audiences at dress rehearsals was discontinued. Even on the concert stage one should protest against injustices!

But such episodes are not uppermost in my mind when I think of Brussels. I associate with that city some of my happiest memories, and not only because of the many gratifying performances I gave there. For me, the city is irrevocably linked with the names of two unique human beings, whose lives became closely interwoven with mine—the incomparable Belgian violinist, Eugène Ysaÿe, and that noble woman, Queen Elisabeth of Belgium.

I came to know Ysaÿe shortly after my Paris debut with Lamoureux. We gave concerts together, and periodically I would play with his orchestra in Brussels—he was, of course, world-famed as a violinist but he was also a splendid conductor, whose orchestra was one of the best in Europe. When we first met he was in his early forties— twenty years my senior—but, in a way, it was as if there were no difference in our ages. We became like brothers. A small brother and a big brother. He was a giant of a man, but a graceful giant who moved with effortless ease—he reminded me of a lion with his majestic head and wonderful eyes. I have never known an artist with a more imposing stage presence. And he had a heart to match his body. He was a man of embracing warmth and magnanimity, with an unquenchable zest for life. He lived to the full—he used to say he burned his candle at both ends—and his music reflected his fiery spirit. When he played, one felt ennobled.

Ysaÿe's career, like mine, began in a way in a café. It was the great Hungarian violinist, Joseph Joachim, who discovered him in a café in Berlin and persuaded him to pursue a concert career. Of course his mode of playing differed greatly from Joachim's. Ysaÿe liberated the violin from the strictures of the past. I cannot agree with those who feel he took too many liberties with a score and couldn't curb his imagination. One has to remember the time at which his artistry developed and the inhibiting traditions of "classicism" he overcame. Indeed, his imaginative powers were integral to his genius, and his influence on the art of the violin has been immeasurable. For me, he remains the greatest violinist of them all. You might say he discovered the true soul of the instrument.

Recently I came on some notes I made a number of years ago about Ysaÿe. This is part of what I wrote:

Once Ysaÿe came into the picture, he outdated all the schools and trends of violin playing of his time.

Ysaÿe was the greatest violinist of his period not because he made more notes than his contemporaries but because he made them better. His influence has lasted irresistibly. The younger generations of violinists continue to be shaped by that influence.

The advent of Ysaÿe was a revelation not only because of his technical mastery but especially because of the qualities of color, accent, warmth, freedom, expressiveness, which he brought to the interpretation of music. He was the first to break down the barriers of the German traditions.

Sometimes I used to visit Ysaÿe at his summer home at Gedinne near the River Meuse. He loved to fish, and I can still see him sitting beside the river with his rod—and his pipe. He relished a pipe and, like me, was rarely without one. But I didn't share Ysaÿe's fondness for fishing; even as a boy I couldn't stand the sight of those beautiful creatures wriggling helplessly when caught. . . .

How tragic it was that this vibrant and magnificent man was fated to ultimately suffer as he did from diabetes and die a crippling, lingering death!

It was at one of my concerts in the early 1900's in Brussels that I first met Queen Elisabeth of Belgium. During the intermission, a messenger came backstage and told me that King Albert and Queen Elisabeth would like me to join them in their box. On that occasion the king presented me with a decoration. Queen Elisabeth was then in her mid-twenties—we were, in fact, the same age. After that, she came to all my concerts in Brussels.

But when I speak of Queen Elisabeth, one of the first things I think of is another public occasion, when an incident occurred that really gives an insight into her character. This happened after we had already known each other for some years, at a conference sponsored by the Royal Institute. The gathering was in a large hall—Jean Cocteau, who was receiving a tribute of some sort, delivered an address about the works of Colette—and again I was invited to the royal box. When I came there, Queen Elisabeth indicated an empty chair beside her and invited me to be seated. I realized the chair was the king's and I hesitated—it was, I knew, against protocol for anyone else to occupy it. But she smiled and said again, pointing to the chair, "Please be seated, Pau." So I sat down. I remained in the king's chair for the rest of the conference. People in the hall kept glancing toward the box, and I later learned that the episode had created something of a scandal. That action of hers was typical. "Protocol is sometimes necessary," she once told me, "but I don't like the word."

Queen Elisabeth was a small fragile-looking woman, but she had a will of iron. When she did something, it was because she believed it the right thing to do. She wanted to stand alone and to decide for herself, no matter what others said. In many ways she was the most unconventional member of royalty I have ever met. But in every way she was queenlike—she had an inner nobility. Perhaps one day someone will write the full story of her life. It would be an inspiring book.

She was born a German princess. Her father, Duke Théodor of Bavaria, was a highly cultured man, whose palace was frequented by writers and artists; he was also, remarkably enough, a distinguished physician. Elisabeth became interested in medicine through him and took a medical degree at the University of Leipzig. She also shared her father's love for the arts. She loved music most of all. It remained a passion with her throughout her life. She herself played the violin well—she studied under Ysaÿe—and in later years she founded an international musical contest in Belgium, the Concours International Reine Élisabeth.

Though German by birth, she became probably the most beloved citizen of her adopted country after her marriage to Prince Albert—they were married at the turn of the century. She was especially concerned about the problems of the working people. She dedicated herself to every sort of social cause; and she founded a medical clinic, at which she herself taught nursing. When the First World War came and the Germans invaded Belgium, she refused to leave. She stayed in Brussels until the Germans were at the gates of the city. Then she retreated with the Belgian army, serving as a nurse. "As long as a single foot of free Belgian soil remains," she said, "I will be on it." When only a few miles of unconquered territory were left, she stayed there, living with King Albert in a little house in a coastal town that was under heavy bombardment—her life was in constant danger. She set up a hospital in an old hotel, where she helped care for the sick and wounded, and she organized a school for the children of refugees. When the Germans at last began to withdraw, she followed on the heels of their retreating army.

In the years after the war, Queen Elisabeth championed

all kinds of liberal causes. Sometimes her conduct shocked the aristocrats, but she did not care. Her greatest concern was world peace, and after the Second World War, she helped sponsor the Stockholm Peace Appeal, calling for the banning of all atomic weapons. She was interested in what happened everywhere in the world. She traveled widely— in Europe, Asia, Africa, America. When she was over eighty, she went to visit Premier Khrushchev in the Soviet Union and Mao Tse-tung in China. Always she had a great love of nature—her knowledge of flowers and trees was like a botanist's—somehow she found time to study birds and to write a scholarly book called *The Songbirds of Laeken.* In the introduction, she wrote: "I dedicate this book to all children, and I urge them to listen to our brothers, the birds."

Our paths were to cross repeatedly for more than sixty years. We never lost touch—never, despite all the vicissitudes of her life and mine, despite the two world wars and the Spanish Civil War. Whenever I went to Belgium, I visited her. I would give recitals for her at the palace, and sometimes she joined me in playing chamber music—she was immensely fond of chamber music and often invited musicians for an evening of trios or quartets. During my exile in Prades she wrote me frequently—her letters were a source of joy and comfort to me. Later she attended my music festivals in Prades and, after I settled in Puerto Rico, the festivals in San Juan and Marlboro, Vermont. In the summer Martita and I would go to Brussels and visit Queen Elisabeth as her guests at the palace. The last time we visited her was in the summer of 1966. A few months later this great spirit died at the age of eighty-nine.

In her will she left a jewel to me as a gift—with the instruction that I was to give the jewel to Martita.

viii

Into the Storm

My father had suffered increasingly from attacks of asthma in the years after I moved to Paris. He never mentioned it in his letters to me, and when I came home for vacations he would make light of his sickness, but I knew from my mother and the doctors how serious it was. The doctors said it was imperative that he move to another climate—he needed mountain air, they said—and I insisted that he act on their advice. I bought him a house in a mountain village called Bonastre, and he went to live there. But his health continued to deteriorate.

In the autumn of 1906, I was in Basel, Switzerland, taking part in a performance of Bach's *St. Matthew Passion*. The great Dutch singer, Johannes Messchaert, was singing one of the most magnificent arias in the work, and I was playing the cello part, when suddenly I was overwhelmed by a terrible feeling. At that moment I knew with dreadful certainty that my father was dying. As soon as the performance was over, I canceled all other engagements of my concert tour, and I left directly for Vendrell. When I arrived, I learned that my beloved father had died on the day I had been playing in Basel. He was buried not far from the church where he had been organist and where, as a child, I had sung while he played.

At the time of my father's death, I had taken up residence in a house in the Auteuil district in Paris. It was one of a cluster of houses for rent on a small estate called the Villa Molitor. In back of the house was a tiny garden—I used to sit there in the early evenings, smoking my pipe. The house became a gathering place for my friends, and a day rarely passed without some of them coming to visit me. We would play chess and talk and sometimes play music together. I was always glad to get back to the Villa Molitor at the end of one of my concert tours.

It was, however, my mother's feeling that I should have a house of my own in Catalonia. "With all the traveling you are doing," she said on one of my summer visits home, "you need a place where you can really rest. You cannot do that in Paris. You need to be here in your own land by the sea." Shortly after my father's death, she suggested we build a house at San Salvador. We bought a number of acres right beside the sea. She designed the house herself— a simple but charming house on the beach where I had spent so many hours as a child—and she made all the arrangements for its construction. She supervised the planting of the gardens and orchards and directed all the operations of the farm. The people who worked on the place had the greatest respect for her—they felt she knew more than the experts.

Every summer I would spend my vacation of two or three months at San Salvador with my mother and my brothers, Luis and Enrique, who were still in their teens. Luis was studying agriculture, and Enrique already showed unusual talent as a violinist. It was a joy for me to be there. I would get up early in the morning and walk along the beach, watching the sun rise over the ocean and stopping to talk with the fishermen. The place had lost none of the fascination it held for me as a child. The moment I returned I had the feeling of being liberated. I have always found in nature an inexhaustible source of sustenance. And my visits to San Salvador provided me with the only real opportunity I had in those days for composing.

What my mother said about my life in Paris was true. Intense activities consumed much of my time. There were of course frequent concerts and musicales, rehearsals and various other obligations. In addition to everything else, I was interested in the work at the École Normale de Musique, which I had helped found together with Thibaud and Cortot. It was a period when I did a great deal of teaching. One of my most talented pupils was Maurice Eisenberg, with whom I was to form a friendship that would prove so precious to me in future years. Anyway, when I returned to Paris from a concert tour, there was little time for relaxation. Usually, in fact, it was just the opposite.

I recall one experience in particular. I cannot say that it was typical—fortunately, I have never had another quite like it. But it does illustrate the sort of thing that could disturb a musician's life in Paris.

It had become a custom of mine to take part in an annual benefit concert for the Lamoureux and Colonne orchestras. On this particular occasion, the date set for the concert was the very day on which I returned to Paris after a lengthy tour. A public rehearsal was scheduled for the morning, as was customary in those days, and though I was tired after a night on the train, I went directly to the concert hall. The conductor, Gabriel Pierné, and I had agreed some weeks previously that I would play the Dvořák concerto. Shortly before the rehearsal was to start, Pierné came to my dressing room to go over the score and discuss my approach to the work. Something in his manner struck me as odd—he seemed almost uninterested in what we were discussing, but I thought he was probably preoccupied with other matters. Then, all at once, he tossed the score down and exclaimed with a grimace, "What a ghastly piece of music!" I thought at first he was being facetious—I couldn't imagine his really meaning such a thing. He was, after all, a composer himself who had studied under Massenet and César Franck. But he added, "It's hardly worth playing. It's not really music at all." He said it in such a way that there was no doubting he was serious.

I stared at him incredulously. "Are you out of your mind?" I said. "How can you talk that way about such a magnificent work?" Didn't he know, I asked, that Brahms considered it a classic and said he himself would have composed a concerto for the cello if he'd known such effects were possible?

Pierné shrugged. "What of it? Was Brahms infallible? You're enough of a musician to know how bad the music is."

I was almost speechless with anger. "If that's the way you feel about the work," I said, "then you're clearly not capable of conducting it. Since I happen to love the music, I couldn't take part in its desecration. And I won't. I refuse to play."

Members of the orchestra began pressing around us. Someone said the hall was full, and it was time to go onstage. Pierné told me, "Well, we have no choice. You'll have to play."

"On the contrary," I said, "I'm going home."

Pierné rushed onstage. He stood there with his hands raised, his hair and beard disheveled. He declared dramatically, "Pablo Casals refuses to play for us today!"

A great commotion broke out in the hall. I wanted to explain what had happened, but I couldn't make myself heard above the din. People started crowding onto the stage, arguing and protesting that they had paid for their tickets. I caught sight of the composer Claude Debussy standing nearby. I told him about the situation. "Ask Debussy," I said to Pierné, "if he thinks any artist could perform under the circumstances."

To my astonishment, Debussy shrugged and said, "If you really wanted to play, you could."

I replied, "That may be your opinion, Monsieur Debussy, but I can tell you I haven't the slightest intention of doing so."

I got my things together and left the hall.

Next day I received a court summons indicating I was being sued for breach of contract. The legal technicalities dragged on for weeks. When the case finally came to court, the prosecutor himself said he thought my conduct was justified from an artistic viewpoint. But of course there are certain discrepancies between the requirements of art and those of the law. The judge ruled against me. I was fined 3,000 francs, which—with the rate of exchange at the time —was no pittance!

I must confess that—court verdict or not—I would act the same way today. Either you believe in what you are doing or you do not. Music is something to be approached with integrity, not something to be turned on or off like tap water.

At the time of my controversy with Pierné, the newspapers in Paris criticized me as being contentious and temperamental. Actually, it is not my nature to seek quarrels. The opposite, I think, is true—I find so much of interest in other people, and especially in their different ways of thinking, that whether I agree with them or not my inclination is not to be argumentative but to try to learn from them. The question of temperament is perhaps more complicated. I suppose most individuals have certain idiosyncrasies— that is doubtless one of the things that make them individuals. Quite often, in fact, during interviews, I have been asked to tell about my own idiosyncrasies. I do not like to disappoint my questioners. I know they would like to hear something startling and unusual. I know they will not be satisfied if I tell them I have a passion for playing dominoes and an addiction to pipe smoking—or that my eyes are very sensitive to light and I carry an umbrella to protect them from the sun. But what else can I tell them? The truth is that I regard myself as a rather plain person with simple likes and dislikes. In music too I seek simplicity—perhaps today that might be considered my chief idiosyncrasy!

It is commonly believed, I know, that eccentricity is part of the artistic temperament, but I do not happen to share this viewpoint. I am sure one can find very erratic individuals among plumbers and bankers; and, at the same time, if it were possible for us to meet Bach or Shakespeare, I think we'd be struck by their lack of eccentricity. Some great composers, of course, have been extremely eccentric. I think of Richard Wagner, for example, and some of the things his friend, the conductor Hans Richter, used to tell me about him—his fiery temper, his arbitrary ways, his egocentricity. However, I do not regard such qualities as essential to his creative genius but as weaknesses toward which one should be tolerant and which have small importance. It is his works, not his idiosyncrasies, that are memorable. Sometimes, indeed, the idiosyncrasies of an artist can seriously hamper his work. An example would be my friend, the Hungarian-born composer Emanuel Moór.

Moór was in my opinion a true genius, one of the really outstanding composers of this century. He was also a magnificent pianist and a remarkable inventor—among his inventions were the double-keyboard piano and a mechanical stringed instrument that included all registers from the double bass to the violin. But his eccentricities were such

that they interfered greatly with the acceptance of his
music.

I became acquainted with Moór's music under dramatic
circumstances. I met him at one of my concerts in Lausanne,
Switzerland, where he was living at the time. A Russian
cellist named Brandukoff introduced him to me as an "amateur composer," but I sensed something remarkable about
him—you could see the man's intensity in his face. I told
him I would like to hear some of his work, and I invited
him to visit me in Paris. He came shortly afterwards to see
me at the Villa Molitor. He brought with him a veritable
mountain of scores. Almost the moment he sat down at the
piano and began to play, I realized he was an artist of immense talent. His music was overwhelming. He played
several of his works, one after the other; and the more he
played, the more convinced I became that he was a composer of the highest order. When he stopped, I said simply,
"You are a genius." He looked at me for a moment in silence, his features working terribly, and suddenly he burst
into tears. Then his story poured from him.

He had started his musical career, he told me, as a pianist
and had met with considerable success on the concert stage.
From the time of his youth, however, he had a consuming
passion to compose. But as the years went by he had found
it almost impossible to secure an audience for his works—
he was constantly told his music was without merit. Finally,
after repeated rebuffs, he gave up in despair and stopped
composing. He had then been in his mid-thirties. For the
last ten years, he said, he had written no music. "But that
is impossible!" I told him. "What you've just played for
me is superb music. You must start composing again." He
seized my hands and said, "I will, I will!"

And he did. He began visiting me regularly each month
in Paris, and every time he brought some new work. His

output was prodigious—he composed at incredible speed. Sometimes he brought a symphony, sometimes an opera, sometimes a group of songs or a piece of chamber music. But always something that bore the mark of his special genius. I undertook to introduce his music to the public. I played works of his at my concerts and persuaded friends of mine—Ysaÿe, Cortot, Bauer, Kreisler and others—to do the same. I also arranged concerts at which I conducted his works, and prevailed upon other conductors to include his compositions in their programs. But I met with constant resistance. And why? One of the chief reasons was Moór's eccentricity.

I never knew a man with a greater capacity for offending people and making enemies. He was peremptory, short-tempered, violently opinionated. If someone disagreed with his opinions, he would savagely turn on them and call them names. I remember one occasion when a well-known pianist came to my house while Moór was there. It was toward evening, and Moór had spent the entire day playing his new compositions to me. But when the other pianist began to play, Moór could scarcely control his exasperation. He listened in glowering silence while the pianist played several of his own transcriptions of Bach, for which he was noted. When the pianist had finished, he turned to Moór and said, "What do you think of those, M. Moór?" Moór burst out, "I think you're an utter idiot!"

Another time I had managed—not without some effort —to arrange for Moór's works to be played at a performance of the Classical Concert Society in London, and we traveled together to England. We went for a rehearsal to the home of the distinguished English pianist, Leonard Borwick —he was a splendid musician who had studied with the famous pianist and teacher, Clara Schumann. While Borwick and I were rehearsing a Beethoven sonata, which was

a Pablo Casals.

Second Concerto

pour

Violoncelle

et

Orchestre

par

Emanuel Moór

op. 64

To my dear friend Pablo Casals
in admiration for his
playing of Bach, without
which I never would
have written this work.

Ouchy 12th Dec: 1905

Long live Casals!!
Em. Moór

The score of a concerto for violoncello dedicated to Casals by Emanuel Moór

one of the works on the concert program, I could see that
Moór was getting increasingly irritated. I motioned to him
to calm down, but to no avail. We began playing the next
work—a Bach sonata—when Moór suddenly strode to the
piano, seized Borwick by the shoulders and thrust him violently off the bench, shouting, "Let me show you how to
play Bach!" Borwick—who was very much of an English
gentleman—simply said to Moór, very quietly, "Thank you,
sir, I shall play to the best of my ability."

Naturally, such conduct did not endear Moór to his
confreres! His very deportment sometimes disturbed people.
His table manners—or, rather, the complete lack of them
—revolted others. I understood that he was a man consumed by music and that if he bolted his food like a raven-
ous animal, it was because music coursed through his brain
at night and lack of sleep and nervousness kept him in a
famished state. I made allowances for Moór's behavior—
even if I was often embarrassed by it—because I knew how
much the poor man suffered. But other musicians did not
share my sympathy for him. They would say to me, "How
can you have anything to do with him? He's unbearable.
We can't stand the sight of him." I would try to explain,
but I could not make them understand. Time and again
their antipathy toward him interfered with the presentation
of his music.

Unfortunately, Moór's works are today practically un-
known. But I do not regard this as any reflection on their
intrinsic merit. There have been periods when the music of
some of the greatest composers has been ignored. Consider
Bach himself—his works were really discovered almost a
century after his death by Mendelssohn. And I can remember the time when Mozart's works were regarded merely
as pleasing divertissements and included in programs just
to fill them up. Genius, however, has a way of asserting it-

self. And I am convinced that one day Moór will come into
his own.

At one of my concerts in Berlin in 1913, I met the well-
known American lieder singer, Susan Metcalfe—she came
backstage after the performance to congratulate me. When
she indicated to me her interest in Spanish songs, I offered
to help her develop a repertoire of them. We worked together during the following months, and the next spring
we were married in New Rochelle, New York, where she
was then living. Afterwards we gave a number of concerts
together in Europe and the United States, at which I played
as her accompanist. We were, however, ill-suited to one
another, and our relationship was short-lived, though it
was some years before we were divorced. Our life together
was not a happy one. But these, of course, are things one
does not discuss.

I think that perhaps the happiest memories of my Paris
days are those associated with the small informal music
sessions at which my friends and I would periodically get
together and play for our own pleasure. Those sessions became a cherished custom with us, you might say a ritual—
though there was nothing ritualistic about them in the
ordinary sense. We usually gathered in the small parlor at
Thibaud's house. Generally four or five of us were present.
Our group included Ysaÿe, Thibaud, Kreisler, Pierre Monteux, Cortot, Bauer, Enesco, myself. Georges Enesco was
the youngest—he had come to Paris from Romania in the
early 1900's when he was about twenty. He was a very
sensitive youth, handsome in a delicate poetic way; he
played both the violin and the piano superbly, and he was
already composing marvelous music. We soon became the
closest of friends.

Those sessions at Thibaud's place would begin in the late spring or early summer, at the end of the concert season, when our tours were finished. Our group would come together, like homing pigeons, from all parts of the globe. Ysaÿe would have just returned from a tour of Russia, Kreisler from the United States, Bauer from the Orient, I perhaps from South America. How we all longed for that moment! Then we would play together for the sheer love of playing, without thought of concert programs or time schedules, of impresarios, box-office sales, audiences, music critics. Just ourselves and the music! We played duets, quartets—chamber music—everything and anything we felt like playing. We understood each other completely. We would constantly change around: Now one would play the first or second violin or viola, now another. Sometimes Enesco would be at the piano, sometimes Cortot. Usually we met after supper, and we would play and play. No one paid the slightest attention to time. The hours flew past—we stopped occasionally for something to eat or drink. Often when we finished, it was early morning as we left Thibaud's.

The time was to come when we would have to discontinue those wonderful sessions at Thibaud's—when our lives, like the lives of millions of others, would be suddenly shaken by the upheaval of 1914. That summer Kreisler was conscripted into the Austrian army. It was hard to imagine that gay and gentle genius in a soldier's uniform. And what a shock when he was one of the first wounded on the Russian front! Bauer would soon move to the United States. Ysaÿe went to live in London. . . .

Occasionally in the war years some members of our group did meet and play together at the home of Muriel Draper, the American socialite who was then living in London. We played in a cellar room which we used to call "the cave." It was a really charming place—there were comfortable chairs, and large cushions scattered all about. But it was never really the same as it had been in Paris. In the back of our minds, there was always the terrible specter of the war.

During the early part of this century most Europeans had seen little of war. The time had not yet come when tens of millions would be familiar with the horrors of trench warfare, the ghastly casualty lists, the flight of women and children from flaming towns. Nor was war, as it is today, a topic of daily conversation, a nightly spectacle on television programs, a bottomless pit for the wealth of great nations.

Though Spain in the early 1900's was no longer one of the great powers, her people were perhaps more closely acquainted with war than other Europeans. My own memory of war dates back to before the turn of the century—to what was called the Disaster of 1898. It was then I witnessed in Barcelona a nightmarish scene that has never left me. That was the year of the Spanish-American War and the final crumbling of the Spanish empire: the loss of its colonies of Cuba, the Philippines and Puerto Rico. Like the rest of the people of Spain, we Catalans of course knew about the military campaigns that had been dragging on in Cuba for several years to suppress the rebellion against Spanish rule—there were, after all, almost a quarter of a million Spanish troops in Cuba at the time. But few Spaniards realized what losses their army was suffering, from the guerrilla warfare in the swamps and jungles and especially from malaria, yellow fever and other tropical diseases. These facts were kept from the people, and while the casualties grew, the newspapers reported sweeping successes. Final victory was constantly predicted. Then suddenly, in the summer of 1898, with the entry of the United States into the war, came the catastrophic denouement. Overnight the whole campaign collapsed. Instead of the promised victory, an utter debacle! I was in Barcelona at the time. Shortly after news of the defeat, transport ships arrived in the port carrying remnants of the Spanish army. For days, thousands of soldiers—the sick, the maimed, and those ravaged by hunger and disease—wandered through the streets of the city. The horror of it! It was like a scene from Goya's "Disasters of War." And for what, I asked myself, for what?

The impact on the Spanish people was immeasurable. From one end of the country to the other, the events in Barcelona were repeated. They were even portrayed in one of the zarzuelas produced that year, a work entitled *Gigantes y Cabezudos*, "Giants and Big-Headed Dwarfs." In it there was a scene depicting a ragged band of returning Spanish soldiers, clustered beside the River Ebro, singing a sorrowful song of love for their native land and of their suffering on the foreign battlefield. . . .

A decade or so later war again affected the lives of many families in Spain, and ours was one of them. This time Spain became embroiled in a war in Morocco. It turned into a long and savage conflict—tens of thousands of troops were sent to fight the Riffs—and there was widespread opposition to the war. It was very strong in Catalonia, especially among the intellectuals and the workers. When I would come home to visit my mother and my brothers, I saw all around me the people's bitter resentment. When the government ordered national mobilization, the workers of Barcelona called a general strike in protest. A fierce struggle took place—it came to be known as "Tragic Week"—and martial law was declared. Many were sentenced to imprisonment by military courts, and some were even executed.

It was a terrible time! In 1912 the government decreed obligatory military service. Up until then it had been possible to purchase military exemption, and I had managed to do this for the older of my two brothers, Luis. But now it could not be done for Enrique, who had recently returned from studying the violin in Prague. He had just turned eighteen and was faced with conscription. I was with my mother in Vendrell at the time. It was then she told Enrique that he was not born to kill or to be killed, and that he should flee the country. He decided to go to Argentina—he would continue his musical career there. I bought him a ticket on a boat bound for South America, and he fled. . . .

Of course, the Spanish-American and Moroccan wars paled beside the war that burst on the world in the summer of 1914. Then it was as if the whole of mankind had suddenly gone mad.

I was in Paris when the war broke out. The city went berserk. One would have thought there might be some awareness of the terrible calamity that had overtaken the country, but no, on the contrary, there was a wildly festive mood. Bands playing martial music, flags flying from every window, bombastic speeches about glory and patriotism! What a macabre masquerade! Who knows how many of those young men who paraded smiling through the streets of Paris died in muddy trenches, or came home crippled for life? And in how many other cities and countries were similar parades taking place?

In the days and months that followed, as one nation after another was drawn into the frightful slaughter, one felt that civilization itself had turned backwards. Every human value was perverted. Violence was enshrined, and savagery replaced rationality. The man who killed the largest number of his fellow men was the greatest hero! All of man's creative genius—all knowledge, science, invention—was concentrated on producing death and destruction. And for what purpose were millions massacred and other millions left homeless and starving? People were told it was a war to make the world safe for democracy. Within a few short years after its end, a dozen of the nations that had fought in it would be gripped by dictatorships, and preparations would be under way for another and even more terrible world war!

During that hideous time of the First World War, I was haunted by the question that had tormented me as a youth in Barcelona when I first became conscious of human misery and man's inhumanity to man—"Was this what man was created for?" Sometimes I felt overwhelmed by horror and hopelessness. For me the life of a single child is worth more than all my music; but, in the midst of the war's madness, it was perhaps mainly through music that I maintained my sanity. Music remained for me an affirmation of the beauty man was capable of producing—yes, man who was now causing such havoc and agony. I recalled how when Europe was ravaged a century before by the Napoleonic wars, Beethoven—tormented as he was by the savage conflict—continued to create his great masterpieces. Perhaps at such a time, when evil and ugliness are rampant, it is more important than ever to cherish what is noble in man. During the war, when some were so blinded by hatred they sought to ban German music, I felt it all the more necessary to play the works of Bach, Beethoven and Mozart, which so exemplify the human spirit and the brotherhood of man. . . .

At the outbreak of the war, I gave up my house in Paris and I began living part of the time in New York City. Each year I made a concert tour of the United States. My American friends urged me to stay there permanently. "You can continue your musical work here in peace," they told me. "And you will be safe. You will not have to face the danger

of submarines at sea." But I could not remain away from
my family and friends in Europe. Each season, as soon as
I had completed my concert tour, I would return to Europe
and visit my mother at San Salvador.

When I was in New York in 1916, there occurred a tragic
event which symbolized for me the waste and madness of
the war. Early that year, my dear friend Enrique Granados
arrived from Barcelona to attend the world première of his
opera, *Goyescas*. Granados had an almost morbid fear of
traveling—especially by sea—and for years he had adam-
antly refused to cross the Atlantic. But in this instance he
had finally been prevailed upon for the first time to make
the voyage, because of the importance of the occasion. He
came with his wife Amparo. When we met in New York he
was very nervous about the approaching performance.
Granados was like a child about his music. He really attached no importance to it—it was just something that
poured out of him—and he always questioned its value. As
with his first opera twenty years before when we were both
youths in Barcelona, he asked me if I would assist him with
the rehearsals. He was so tense during the rehearsals at the
Metropolitan Opera House that he never said a word except
when someone addressed a question to him. He didn't speak
English, and so when one of the musicians would ask him
what interpretation he would prefer in some portion of the
work, I would translate the question. Granados would answer, "Just tell them to play whatever way they think best."
It was typical of him. He felt that musicians playing his
works should decide for themselves what would be the best
rendition. The music was of course marvelous, and I tried
to relieve my friend's anxiety by telling him what an immense success the opera would be. On the opening night he
saw for himself! The opera received a tumultuous ovation,
one of the most amazing I have ever witnessed. People in
the audience stood and shouted and wept.

Granados was due to sail home shortly afterwards, but he postponed his trip when he received an invitation from President Wilson to play at the White House. He and his wife set sail for Europe early in March. Two weeks later I heard the terrible news. The ship on which they were crossing the English Channel had been torpedoed. My gentle Granados perished with his wife. He was just forty-nine years old, and at the peak of his creative powers. . . .

Paderewski and Kreisler were in New York at the time, and the three of us decided to give a memorial concert together for the benefit of the Granados children. There were six children—one of them was my godchild—and we knew our friend had left little money. The concert took place at the Metropolitan Opera House, where Granados had triumphed so short a time before. How many people came to attend I could not say. It was raining that night, but when I arrived at the opera house, thousands who could not get seats were standing in the streets.

Walter Damrosch conducted, and Paderewski, Kreisler and I played the Beethoven Trio in B Flat. The famous singers Maria Barrientos, Julia Culp and John McCormack also took part in the concert.

Toward the end of the concert all the lights were turned out. A candle was placed on the piano. Then—with that solitary flame flickering on the stage in the great hall—Paderewski played Chopin's Funeral March.

ix

Music in Barcelona

I returned to Paris for a visit shortly after the end of the war. It was an experience in which joy and sadness were strangely mingled. That jewel of a city evoked in me innumerable vivid memories. All about me as I walked its lovely boulevards and narrow streets were places that had been a dear and familiar part of my life. Here I had come as a young man to seek my career and had made my debut with Lamoureux at the turn of the century. Here I had first met Harold Bauer, Colonel Picquart, Cortot, Thibaud, and so many other treasured friends. Though five years had elapsed since I had lived in Paris, I felt as if it had been only yesterday. And yet, at the same time, that yesterday had a remote and dreamlike quality. It belonged, I knew, to a past that could not be recovered.

At the outbreak of the war, when I had given up my house at the Villa Molitor, I had packed many of my belongings in boxes and stored them in a small warehouse before leaving Paris. Now I went to collect them. I was dismayed at what I found. A scene of dreadful disorder! The boxes had been broken into—my books, musical works and correspondence were scattered all over the floor. Most of the correspondence was gone. Among it, scores of letters from dear friends and former colleagues and acquaintances of mine—from Granados, Saint-Saëns, Richard Strauss, Julius Röntgen, Emanuel Moór and many others. These letters were very dear to me—voices that spoke of precious days and intimate thoughts we had shared—and I felt sickened at the idea of strange hands intruding among them. It was, I was given to understand, the work of the police. They had searched my belongings and taken whatever they desired. Of what I was suspected I still do not know—perhaps my being a foreigner was enough. In wartime anything is possible. In the hope of recovering my letters, I addressed several communications to the French government authorities. Perhaps, I thought, my letters were stored away in their official files. Perhaps they still are. Not long ago a friend of mine tried to intervene with the French writer, André Malraux, when he was Minister of Culture under de Gaulle, to find out if my letters were in the police files, but to no avail. At any rate, I never heard from the authorities or saw my letters again. . . .

Throughout the twenty years in which I had lived abroad, I had known that sooner or later I would make my home again in Catalonia. Periodically, during my visits to San Salvador, my mother and I discussed the question of when I would return to stay. "You will know," she would say, "when the right time comes."

In 1919 I knew that the time had come.

That autumn I once more took up residence in Barcelona, and now I entered a phase of my career which I regard, in many ways, as the most fruitful of my life.

In Barcelona, at the time of my return, there were two symphony orchestras. They had no regular concert schedules—they played only on special occasions and rehearsed infrequently. When I heard them, I thought it was shocking that a city this size did not have something better to offer. Other major European cities had first-class orchestras. Why not Barcelona?

I asked the conductor of one of the orchestras if steps couldn't be taken to improve the situation. He said, "You've been away too long. You don't know Barcelona any more. There isn't the talent for a better orchestra." I went to the conductor of the other orchestra. The answer was the same.

I told both conductors I'd be glad to cooperate in any way I could. If they wished, I said, I'd play for them. If more financial backing were needed, I would raise it. They were not interested.

Originally I had not the slightest intention of forming an orchestra of my own. True, I had a passion for conducting that dated back, I think, to the time I sang in my father's choir; and over the years I had conducted in Paris, London, New York, Vienna and other cities. The cello had never given me full satisfaction, any more than it does now. Not merely because of the endless work and the hateful nervousness before performances. But also because of the instrument's limitations. The one instrument without limitations is the orchestra. It encompasses all others. Early in my career I wrote my friend, the composer Julius Röntgen, "If I've been so happy up until now scratching the cello, think how happy I'll be when I possess that greatest of all instruments—the orchestra!" But not until I met with that rebuff from the two conductors in Barcelona had I really thought of forming my own orchestra. Then I decided, "All right, if they won't build a good orchestra, I'll do it myself!"

Making the decision was one thing—carrying it out was another. I expected certain problems, but I had no idea of the difficulties I'd encounter. The present has an inertia of its own, and there are always people who regard change as if it were a personal threat! I found opposition in almost

Fritz Kreisler, Harold Bauer, Walter Damrosch (seated in chair), and
Casals in New York City in 1918

every quarter to my idea of starting a new orchestra in Barcelona. Wherever I sought cooperation—among professors at the music schools, composers, civic leaders—I was told another orchestra wasn't wanted or it wasn't feasible. The press carried articles ridiculing my idea. Practically no one was willing to offer financial backing. One wealthy man told me, "I prefer bullfighting to music anyway."

As the weeks passed, my frustration mounted. The only encouragement came from my mother, my brother Enrique, and a handful of close friends. Even some of the latter said I was quixotic to continue the struggle. But Don Quixote of course was himself a native of Spain. Anyway, I kept tilting at the windmill!

If I couldn't raise the necessary funds to start the orchestra, I decided, I'd provide them myself, out of my savings. I went to the musicians' union and asked them what they currently earned. The figure was appallingly low. "How can a family live on that?" I asked. They said, "We have to work at other jobs. It is the only thing possible in Barcelona." I told them, "All right, we'll change that. Every musician in my orchestra will receive double that amount."

I combed the city for musicians—I auditioned them by the dozens. Few had had orchestral experience; some had never played professionally; but that was not my criterion. I selected my musicians on the basis of their potentialities. Finally, I had chosen eighty-eight. They formed the embryo of the Orquestra Pau Casals.

It was natural for me to use the Catalan name "Pau" in preference to the Spanish "Pablo." When I was young, it was still the custom in Catalonia to use Spanish baptismal names. And so I'd been called Pablo. But I later came to much prefer my Catalan name—Catalan, after all, is the true language of my people. More than once I'd told my managers I wanted to use the name "Pau" in my concert tours. But they'd argue, "Audiences have come to think of you as Pablo Casals. Nobody will know who Pau Casals is." But now, in naming my own orchestra, I no longer felt under this restriction.

I told the eighty-eight musicians I had picked, "We will become an orchestra that will bring to our city music worthy of the people of Catalonia!"

My understanding with the musicians was that we would rehearse twice daily—at nine in the morning and five in the afternoon. But on the very day before the date set for our first rehearsal, a calamity overtook me. The strain of the previous months of organizing, with all the frustrations and petty details, had been too much. There had been too many sleepless nights, too many anxious days. I fell ill—the doctors said I had collapsed from nervous exhaustion. My illness was complicated by an unfortunate episode. I had difficulty with an eye irritation—my irises were badly inflamed—and a famous oculist treated me. He gave me an injection of some sort. Almost the moment he did so, my head fell to one side and I couldn't move it. I began to perspire so much that my mattress was soaked. A few hours later the doctor's nurse came and gave me a second injection—she didn't know I'd already had one. Then I could not move at all. When my family saw how sick I was, they called our own physician. He was astounded when he learned about the injections—he said the dosage I'd received was enough to kill a horse! And so, with my orchestra finally ready to start work, I was confined to my bed in a helpless condition.

I knew that to cancel the first rehearsal would be psychologically the worst possible thing to do—if I failed at this crucial moment to go ahead as planned, the whole orchestra was likely to fall apart. I didn't inform the musicians of my illness until they were gathered at the concert hall. Then I sent a message asking them to keep assembling each day until I was able to join them.

When the first week was over, I saw that all the orchestra members were paid their salaries. They continued meeting without me for a second week. A delegation then came to see me. "Maestro," they said, "we cannot go on with this arrangement. You are spending a fortune. We cannot accept your money and do nothing."

I knew how much depended on my answer. I told them, "I appreciate your coming. But I must insist on its being this way. You keep your end of the contract, and I'll keep mine. The orchestra should continue to meet daily at nine and five until I'm well enough to conduct rehearsals." I wanted them to realize how serious I was about the whole undertaking.

And so, day after day, while I remained bedridden, they continued to meet. Sometimes they would discuss different compositions; occasionally Enrique—he was first violinist —conducted some work. The days stretched into weeks. . . .

At the end of two months, when it was time for summer vacation, I'd recovered sufficiently to go and address the orchestra. I thanked them for the faith they had shown in me and told them I looked forward to working with them in the fall. Now, I knew, they understood I was serious.

That fall we began rehearsing in earnest. Those musicians who were inexperienced in orchestral playing had much to learn; and those with some experience had—because of bad habits to overcome—perhaps to learn even more! The only solution was work. At the outset I spent hours and hours on a rudimentary orchestral exercise. I took Wagner's "Ride of the Valkyries"—a work which many of the musicians knew by rote and were accustomed to play carelessly and out of tune—and I went over it with them again and again, until they came to understand the importance of being conscious of every note and treating it with respect.

I also stressed that each musician must learn to play, on the one hand, as if he were a soloist and, on the other, with the constant awareness of being an indispensable part of a team. It is this quality of human teamwork—the sense of being one of a group working together to achieve the ulti-mate in beauty—that has always afforded me a joy as a conductor that no solo performance can duplicate.

"We share a great privilege," I told the musicians, "the privilege of bringing masterpieces to life. We also share a sacred responsibility. We are entrusted with the duty of interpreting these masterpieces with utter integrity."

To be a true conductor, one must interpret truly. Above all, a conductor must fully understand the work he is per-forming—he must understand not only all of its technical aspects, and the role of every instrument, but also the music's inner meaning and the nature of the work as a whole. That understanding cannot be static but, like life itself, must constantly grow. No matter how often I have conducted a work, I study it intensively in preparation for each performance, annotating the score for days and some-times weeks before the rehearsals, as if I were conducting the work for the first time. And invariably I discover some-thing new. With my own orchestra, of course, I followed this procedure.

But mastery of the music is in itself not enough. A con-ductor must be able to impart his thoughts to the musicians —not by imposing his will on them but by convincing them of the value of his concepts. It is not only what you say that is important but also how you say it. The most profound truth can sometimes be wasted if it is expressed rudely or arrogantly. One must recognize and respect the feelings of the musicians. "You are not servants of mine," I told the members of my orchestra. "We are all servants of the music."

We gave our first concert in October of that year. I approached the affair with considerable anxiety. When I saw the audience, my heart sank. How many empty chairs there were in the Palau de la Música Catalana! But the reaction of the audience was enthusiastic, and the critics expressed surprise at the quality of the music.

And so my orchestra was launched.

Success did not come overnight. We had a long struggle —intensive work with our music and many organizational problems. We gave two series of concerts a year—one in the spring, one in the autumn. In the winters I continued my own concert tours, giving performances on the cello and occasionally appearing as a guest conductor. Those tours now served a special purpose—they helped provide for my orchestra. Despite growing support from the community, seven years elapsed before the orchestra was fully self-sustaining. In the meantime, I made up each season's deficit.

But each season more and more music lovers rallied to our support. And the day came, in fact, when those very journals that had once scoffed at the idea of the orchestra were boasting it was one of Barcelona's outstanding cultural institutions and had made the city known as a center for symphonic music. If I mention this with pride, it is not from personal vanity. There were eighty-nine of us who produced the music!

I think I can say that we fulfilled our pledge of bringing to Barcelona music worthy of our people. There were rarely vacant seats at our concerts. Looking at those wonderful audiences, I sometimes thought of the persons who had said the citizens of Barcelona wanted only café music!

Bureau International de Concerts C. KIESGEN et E. C. DELAET
—— 47, RUE BLANCHE, 47 ——
Par entente avec M. A. DANDELOT, représ. excl. de M. J. Thibaud, 83, rue d'Amsterdam

THÉATRE DES CHAMPS-ÉLYSÉES

ANNÉE 1923   13, Avenue Montaigne   ANNÉE 1923

PROGRAMMES
DES
S I X
CONCERTS

Alfred CORTOT

Jacques THIBAUD

Alfred CORTOT
Jacques THIBAUD
Pablo CASALS

PRIX :
1 franc.

PRIX :
1 franc.

Pablo CASALS

Program of a concert series given by Casals, Alfred Cortot and Jacques Thibaud at the Théâtre des Champs-Élysées, Paris, 1923

Occasionally, my mother attended the concerts, but she came rarely. It made her suffer to be there, because she knew how nervous I was. She would wait up for me to come home after the performances. And then she would simply say, "Are you satisfied, Pablo?" I would say, "Yes, Mother." And then she would sleep. . . .

My orchestra's programs consisted to a considerable extent of the classics—the great works of Beethoven, Bach, Haydn, Mozart, Brahms, Schumann. But we also frequently played outstanding contemporary works, and I made a special point of including in our programs the music of modern Spanish and Catalan composers—Granados, Albéniz, Manuel de Falla, Juli Garreta, and others.

Of these contemporary composers, I think that in many ways the most unusual was Juli Garreta. In some music encyclopedias you will not even find his name, but he was a phenomenon, a genius of the rarest sort. I can think of no other composer who with his type of background produced such works as Garreta's. He never had a single lesson in his life—he was absolutely self-taught. He came from Sant Feliu de Guixols, a little seaside town about three hours from Barcelona. As a young man he had been a common laborer and then he had taken up the trade of clockmaking. But music was his passion. How he acquired his profound knowledge of music is to me almost incomprehensible— though, of course, he did hear church music and traveling musicians, and he studied every score he could get his hands on. He had a little room near his clock shop, and he would retire to it whenever possible and stay there writing music by the hour. Some of his works were extraordinary—with a universal quality. The music of Granados, one might say, shows especially the influence of Madrid and Andalusia— it is music of Spanish derivation, that is. But much of Garreta's work is above national origin, pure music of the highest order. He wrote many sardanas, lovely sardanas, but he also wrote songs, chamber music, symphonic works: works of major scope, marvelous in structure and melodic content. He had an incredible facility. Naturally, his clock business suffered—the clocks sat unrepaired on his shelves while he composed. Finally he lost all his customers. He moved to Barcelona, and, in order to eat, he got a job playing a piano in a cabaret. It was then I met him. We became greatly attached to one another. He was a very small, quiet man—as quiet as a mouse and as timid. He dressed very neatly, though he had perhaps only one suit of clothes. Sometimes I visited the cabaret where Garreta played. It was a third-rate cabaret, noisy and smoke-filled with a tawdry atmosphere. I never wanted to go there—it made me feel like weeping to see that wonderful artist playing in such a place. When not at the cabaret, he could always be found composing in the nearby, shabbily furnished room where he lived. What music poured out of that little man! I introduced a number of his works with my orchestra. He would bring me compositions he had finished and shyly give them to me for my comment. When I conducted one of his works, he would come to the concert, and the next night he would be back at the cabaret. Without Garreta's knowledge, I arranged for the orchestra to pay him a certain sum of money each month to help him and his wife exist. His wife continued to get the pension after he died.

There was in Juli Garreta the seed of a great master—a seed that never fully flowered because it lacked proper nurturing. I have always believed that if Garreta had had some outstanding teacher, he might have developed into another Brahms or Beethoven. He died when he was in his late forties, at the height of his creativity. . . .

Some of the most memorable of my orchestra's concerts were directed by guest conductors. Fritz Busch, Koussevitzky, Richard Strauss, Pierre Monteux, Klemperer, Stravinsky, Arnold Schoenberg, and other eminent conductors and composers came to Barcelona at my invitation. I derived a particular pleasure from their concerts, and also from those that featured the performances of distinguished guest artists—some of whom were old friends and colleagues of mine, like Thibaud, Cortot, Kreisler and Harold Bauer.

Of all such concerts, the one that stands out most sharply in my memory took place in the spring of 1927 during the music festival we held in Barcelona to commemorate the hundredth anniversary of the death of Beethoven. Several months before, I had visited my dear friend, Eugène Ysaÿe, in Brussels. He was then almost seventy and had stopped playing the violin. His last public performance, in fact, had been very disappointing. I knew he grieved over this fact, and when I saw him, I thought how wonderful it would be if he could take part in the Beethoven centennial. I was convinced he was still capable of a magnificent performance. So I said to him, "Eugène, you must come and play the Beethoven violin concerto at our festival."

He stared at me in astonishment. "But, Pablo," he said, "that's impossible!"

"Why?"

"I haven't played the Beethoven concerto in fourteen years."

I told him, "No matter. You can play."

"You really believe so?"

"I know it. You can and you will."

His face looked suddenly youthful. He said, "Perhaps the miracle will happen!"

And he agreed to make the effort.

Several weeks after I had returned to Barcelona, I received a letter from Ysaÿe's son Antoine. He was greatly disturbed. He questioned whether I should ever have raised his father's hopes that he might play again. "If only you

Casals' friend and colleague, the great Belgian violinist Eugène Ysaÿe

could see my dear father," he wrote, "if you could see him working every day, playing scales slowly and laboriously hour after hour. It is a tragedy, and we cannot help weeping over it." The letter wrung my heart. Had I done the right thing, after all? Still, deep inside me, I felt Ysaÿe would play again.

The time came for the festival, and Ysaÿe arrived in Barcelona. He was terribly nervous at the rehearsal, and—though I was careful not to show it—I was worried too. And when I took my place on the podium on the evening of Ysaÿe's performance and looked at him, I was filled with apprehension. He moved so slowly—he seemed weary—and suddenly I thought, He is old, have I done my friend a great injustice?

I lifted my baton, and he raised his violin to his chin . . . and, with the first notes, I knew that all was well! In some passages it seemed he might falter, and I felt his nervousness throughout. But there were many moments of the great Ysaÿe, and the effect as a whole was overwhelming.

Once again, as so often in the past, I was lost in the wonder of his music. The ovation at the end was frenzied. Then Ysaÿe took my place on the podium and conducted Beethoven's "Eroica" Symphony and afterwards the Triple concerto with Cortot, Thibaud and me playing. . . .

In the dressing room after the concert Ysaÿe was overcome with emotion. He kissed my hands and wept, exclaiming "Resurrection!"

The next day I saw my friend off at the station. He was leaning out of the carriage window talking to me and clasping my hands as the train started slowly to move. He kept hold of me is if he didn't want us to separate, and I moved along the platform with the train. Then, as it gathered speed, he suddenly thrust something into my hands. The train pulled away with Ysaÿe waving from the window.

Then I saw what I was holding, and I knew at that moment that he had wanted to leave with me something—anything —which was, you might say, a part of himself. I was holding Ysaÿe's pipe.

In spite of the success that had come to the Orquestra Pau Casals, there was one thing about our concerts that continued to disturb me. Our music, I felt, reached too limited an audience—largely those who were comfortably off, well-to-do. The working people, generally speaking, could not afford the concert tickets. Those few who could scrape together the money sat in the cheapest gallery seats, and I felt that when they looked down on the gentry luxuriously seated in the stalls and boxes they were likely to be distracted by thoughts that had little to do with music. The idea of giving free concerts didn't appeal to me. I was conscious of the dignity of working people, and I knew they had little desire to receive what might seem charity. I wanted the men and women from the factories and the shops and the waterfront to be able to hear our music and enjoy it. After all, they were the people who had produced most of the wealth of our country—why, then, should they be kept from sharing its cultural riches?

My thoughts on the subject had been influenced by the achievements of that remarkable Catalan patriot and lover of music, José Anselmo Clavé. Clavé had died in 1874, two years before I was born, but I felt toward him as if he had been my close friend. He came from the working class and was a weaver by trade. He played the guitar and taught himself to compose music and songs. His songs dealt with simple, tender themes—with experiences of poor children, with stories about peasants and fishermen, with the beauty of nature and love of Catalonia. Gradually his songs became known among Barcelona workers, and small groups began meeting in the factories to sing them after working hours. Clavé knew what bleakness and poverty existed for the working class, and he wanted to help bring some beauty into their lives. He conceived the idea of organizing permanent choral groups among the workers. And he achieved fantastic results. Under his inspiration, wonderful choral societies of workers and their families evolved not only in Barcelona but in towns throughout Catalonia. Their membership grew into thousands, and their movement had a major impact on the cultural awakening then under way in Catalonia. Such world-famous choral societies as the Orfeó Català and the Orfeó Gracienc were part of the legacy of Clavé's work. This worker-musician became so popular that when he was in his early forties he was elected governor of Tarragona!

After Clavé's death, a statue was erected to his memory in the Plaza de Cataluña in Barcelona. When I passed it, I would think of this good man and his splendid accomplishments. I asked myself—if Clavé had organized choral societies among the workers, would it not be possible to create a workingmen's society for concert music? A plan for such an organization took shape in my mind.

Once my orchestra was on a sound footing, I moved to implement my plan. I visited a workers' night school which sponsored occasional cultural activities among the unions, and I told the school's officials about my ideas for bringing concert music to working people. They listened very politely, but I sensed a certain skepticism in their attitude. A few days later a small delegation of workers came to see me— they came directly from their jobs, still wearing their overalls and blouses. They asked very probing questions. They wanted especially to know who would direct and control the organization I envisioned.

I told them, "It will be run entirely by you. I will simply

put my orchestra at your disposal for a specified number of concerts each year. Also, I will play for you myself and arrange for the appearance of other soloists."

"Who will pay for this?"

"You will."

"How?"

"Your concert association will charge a membership fee of six pesetas a year," I told them—six pesetas then amounted to about a dollar. "This will entitle the members to attend the special concerts given by my orchestra."

"And all of this for six pesetas?"

"Yes, all for six pesetas."

The delegation went away. They discussed my plan with the unions and other workers' organizations. It was decided to give the plan a trial. An organization was established called Associació Obrera de Concerts—the Workingmen's Concert Association. The qualifications for joining were simple: Membership was restricted to those whose monthly earnings were less than five hundred pesetas—which was about a hundred dollars in those days.

The Orquestra Pau Casals gave its first workers' concert on a Sunday morning in the fall of 1928 at the Olympia Theater in Barcelona. More than two thousand workers crowded into the concert hall. When I looked at those rows of simply dressed men and women waiting for the concert to start, I felt an indescribable elation. At the end of the performance, the entire audience arose and gave the orchestra a thunderous ovation. Then they started chanting my name. Those shouts of the working people of Barcelona, I think, meant more to me than any applause I had ever received.

My orchestra began giving a series of six Sunday morning concerts a year for the Workingmen's Concert Association. Its membership grew at an amazing rate. Branches of the Association, and choral groups affiliated with it, sprang up all over Catalonia.

At one point I suggested that the Association publish a music periodical of its own.

"Who will write for it?" they asked.

"Your members."

"And about what?"

"About their reactions to the music they hear at the concerts and similar subjects."

They began publishing a magazine called *Fruicions*. And not only were they astonished by the results—I was too! These were the titles of some articles in a typical issue: "The Relation of Art and Ideas," "The Late Quartets of Beethoven," "Stravinsky and Rhythm," "In Appreciation of Schubert."

Within a few years after the Association's formation, when the Spanish Republic had come into being, the organization had its own music library and its own music school—which Enrique and I helped establish. The Association formed its own orchestra, composed entirely of workers, and gave concerts on Sundays in Barcelona and other industrial centers of Catalonia—sometimes they performed in hospitals and prisons. Musicians, critics and musicologists came from other countries to study the Association and its activities.

My orchestra's concerts for the Association became so popular that when we began holding daytime concerts during the working week, government offices would close down so that their employees might attend the performances.

By then the membership of the Association and its affiliates numbered in the tens of thousands in Catalonia. I used to say that if I had wanted to make a revolution using only the Association members, we could doubtless have seized power!

If the accomplishments of the Workingmen's Concert Association gave me great happiness—and no musical undertaking has ever given me more—there were other aspects of the lives of Catalan workers in those postwar years which caused me deep distress. During the early 1920's there was widespread unemployment and social unrest in Catalonia. Many went hungry—you saw beggars everywhere. When workers' demonstrations and strikes broke out in Barcelona and other cities, the Spanish government took harsh measures to suppress them. Once again martial law was instituted. Many workers were imprisoned or deported. The situation was aggravated when the Spanish army suffered a series of catastrophic defeats in Morocco—almost twenty thousand soldiers were killed by the Riff tribes led by Abd-el-Krim. Protests against the war swept Catalonia. On every side you heard the demand that the *responsabili-dados*—the "responsible ones"—be brought to account. More and more people spoke out for the independence of Catalonia and the right to determine their own destiny. Instead there came the military dictatorship of Primo de Rivera and with it, during the next years, more repressions, more imprisonments, more Catalan patriots sent into exile —among them the great Catalan leader who is now a legend, Colonel Francesc Maciá. The population seethed with resentment.

It was inevitable that my own thoughts and work were affected by this atmosphere—one cannot, of course, separate music from life. My support of Catalan autonomy was well known, and on one occasion I was involved in an episode that almost precipitated a national scandal.

The spark that set off this incident was a speech that King Alfonso delivered during a visit to Barcelona. It was a very foolish speech. In it he referred to himself as the successor to King Philip V of Spain, who was especially despised by Catalans because he had robbed Catalonia in the eighteenth century of many of her ancient liberties. The citizens of Barcelona were outraged by Alfonso's words. I myself was greatly disturbed. Perhaps, I thought, he hadn't realized their implication—perhaps he had been ill-advised. Shortly afterwards, on one of my periodic visits to the palace in Madrid, I decided to tell the Queen Mother, María Cristina, about the anger in Barcelona and to urge that Alfonso do something to rectify his mistake. But when I brought up the subject, Queen María Cristina hardly seemed to hear what I was saying. She quickly switched the conversation into other channels and began asking me about my concert tours and my orchestra. I left the palace with a feeling of dejection and foreboding.

However, not much later—and perhaps, indeed, because my talk with Doña María Cristina had more effect than I realized—King Alfonso did make what seemed a conciliatory gesture toward the people of Catalonia. It was announced that he and his wife, Queen Victoria—she was the granddaughter of the British Queen Victoria—would attend the opening of the International Exposition being held that year in Barcelona. Prior to Alfonso's arrival, I received a message from him saying he would like to come to one of my orchestra's concerts and would appreciate the program's including a cello performance by me. Though I ordinarily did not play at concerts of the Orquestra Pau Casals, I made arrangements to comply with his request.

The audience that gathered at the Liceu Opera House that evening included members of the court, leading government officials, high army officers, and the social élite of Barcelona. The first half of the program was concluded before the arrival of the royal party. Toward the end of the intermission I received word backstage that the king and queen and their entourage were about to enter the theater. I was asked to conduct the Royal March—which was then the Spanish anthem. Since I was about to play the cello, I felt it appropriate that Enrique conduct the anthem and requested him to do so. Immediately there was a great to-do. My failing to lead the orchestra, I was told, could be construed as an affront to Their Majesties. Emissaries scurried back and forth while the royal party waited outside the theater and the intermission was prolonged. It was finally agreed to proceed as I had suggested.

When the king entered the hall, he was greeted by only a scattering of applause. There was a perceptible chill in the atmosphere. I had a presentiment that something drastic was about to happen. And it did! The moment I stepped onstage with my cello, pandemonium broke loose. Throughout the auditorium people rose to their feet, applauding and shouting. Ladies waved their handkerchiefs. The audience kept applauding until the royal party too arose in their box. Then, all at once, someone in the audience shouted, "Casals is *our* king!" I stood there not knowing what to do. I was terribly embarrassed. I knew of course that this was not really an ovation for me— it was a political demonstration. As the uproar continued, police officers appeared and hustled a number of demonstrators from the hall. Gradually the hubbub subsided, and I was able to proceed with my performance. Whenever members of the royal family had attended past performances of mine, I had been invited to join them in their box at the end of the concert. This time there was no invitation.

I was extremely upset afterwards. Not only did the incident constitute an insult to the king but he was, after all, my guest at the concert. I was saddened too by the thought that this might mean the end of my friendship with the royal family. At the same time, of course, I could not apologize. I knew how the Catalans still felt about Alfonso's reference to King Philip V, and I shared that feeling.

Some weeks later a remarkable thing happened. I was in Paris when the Spanish ambassador came to see me. He told me that King Alfonso wanted me to give a cello performance in Madrid on the occasion of a state visit by King Victor Emmanuel and Queen Elena of Italy. I gladly consented. The concert—it was held in the sumptuous Hall of Arms—was a most impressive affair. The hall, lit by candlelight, was filled with ladies in beautiful gowns, officers in colorful uniforms, and members of the various diplomatic corps. Seated in the front row of the audience were the royal families of Spain and Italy. When I had played my concluding work, Alfonso came up and engaged me in conversation. In accordance with protocol, the audience remained standing while he stood and talked. He kept on talking, about all sorts of things—about the games we'd played together when he was a small boy, about my mother, about my brothers, Luis and Enrique. And all this time, the other members of the Spanish royal family, the King and Queen of Italy, and all the assembled dignitaries stood— as if at attention. I realized that Alfonso was doing this deliberately. Finally, with a smile, he said to me, "Pablo, I want you to know how happy I was to see how much the Catalan people love you." With that, he turned and walked away.

The next day the newspapers were full of the story of how the king had kept everyone standing while he talked to me—it created quite a scandal. After all, I was only a musician, and a Catalan at that! But I knew it was Alfonso's way of acknowledging the mistake of his speech in Barcelona and of saying that we understood one another.

X

San Salvador

I have read accounts of my life that give the impression that all of my days have been devoted to ceaseless work—to unrelieved practicing, performing, conducting, composing. I am afraid I cannot claim to have been such a paragon of labor. True, I have done my share of work— my cello is a demanding tyrant—but I have also had my share of relaxation, athletics and recreation. Since childhood I have not confined my playing to musical instruments! Some of my most enjoyable hours have been spent playing tennis, horseback riding, swimming, mountain climbing— and, more recently, at the pastime of dominoes. In spite of the demands made upon me by my duties with the Orquestra Pau Casals and my continuing concert tours, I still found time for other, less arduous forms of self-expression. They were, in fact, made possible by the proximity of San Salvador, where I had my beloved beach and my own tennis court.

My favorite sport at the time really was tennis. I had played a lot of tennis during the years in which I lived in Paris. We used to have our own annual contest among the musicians—Ysaÿe, Cortot, Thibaud and others. My doubles partner was an organist named Kelly; he played like a professional, and I myself was very fast on the court, and we always won the doubles championship. When I traveled to England, I used to visit Ridgehurst, the country estate of Sir Edward Speyer, the British financier and famous patron of music, who helped found the Classical Concert Society —he was already almost seventy when we met, a wonderful old man, who had been friends with Joachim, Brahms, and other great musical figures. Speyer was a tennis enthusiast himself; he had a splendid court at Ridgehurst, and I always took my racket as well as my cello with me when I went there. In his memoirs Speyer recalls my arriving at his estate one day in the early 1900's—dressed in my white flannels—and saying, "First we'll play six sets of tennis and then the two Brahms sextets."

There were a number of fine tennis players who came to San Salvador, but I think the best of all was a Catalan girl, Panchita Subarina. She was then only fifteen or so, but she was marvelous! She was the best woman player I ever saw, and she went on to win many championships. Interestingly enough, we met again not long ago—some forty years after playing tennis together in San Salvador—when I attended a music festival in Israel. She had married an Israeli citizen and settled in Tel Aviv.

Tennis was to remain a passion with me over the years. I have continued to follow the game closely—I have known three generations of champions, beginning with such great players as Jean Borotra, who was called the "bounding Basque." One of the last games I played was with my godson, Pablo Eisenberg, when he came with his parents to visit me in Prades in 1947—he was a junior champion at the time. I was then seventy-one. . . .

When living abroad, I had always longed for my summer vacations at San Salvador. But after my return to Catalonia the house there really became my home. Though I still spent many weeks each year on tour and much time in Barcelona with my orchestra, I not only passed the summers at San Salvador but visited it whenever I could. And what a joy it was to be there, with my mother and Luis and his family, and the beauty of the sea at my door!

As a boy, I had loved to ride horseback. Now I had a horse of my own. His name was Florian. He was a magnificent animal—an Andalusian Arab, large, jet-black, with excellent gaits. In the early mornings I would ride him along the beach, galloping to the music of the wind and the surf. We had a splendid comradeship. It was about two hundred yards from the house to his stable, but the moment I came out of the house in the early morning he would hear me and whinny in excitement. I had him from a colt, and he lived to be twenty-four years old.

The other animals on our farm—geese, ducks, cows, burros, doves—were also a constant source of delight to me. Different personalities, all of them. There was one small burro of whom I was especially fond. He was so gentle, so friendly and intelligent—those who call burros stupid simply do not know these animals. I used to bring this burro into the house to bid good-morning to my young nieces and nephews. I think he relished this ceremony no less than the children did!

I had canaries too—eight of them in separate cages along the hallway leading to the small music room containing the piano that had belonged to my father. Each dawn when I had arisen and was about to commence the day by playing Bach at my father's piano, I would be greeted by their song. They would start singing the moment they heard my footsteps on the stairs, and they would continue their chorus while I played. Sometimes it seemed to me that I was their accompanist.

Alas, not all the memories of my animal friends at San

Salvador are such happy ones. I had a dog, a German shepherd named Follet, who was like my shadow. He slept outside, but he knew my schedule to the minute, and when I left the house for my morning ride, he would be waiting for me on the doorstep. Then a terrible thing happened. One morning I opened the door, and there lay Follet in a pool of blood. He was dead. A trail of blood led all the way from his body to the front gate. During the night somebody had tried to force the gate open, and when Follet had apparently tried to guard it, the prowler had stabbed him, wounding him horribly. He had crawled from the gate to the front door, and there he had waited for me to the end. Such was the faithfulness of my friend.

There are, I know, people who do not love animals, but I think this is because they do not understand them—or because, indeed, they do not really see them. For me, animals have always been a special part of the wonder of nature—the smallest as well as the largest—with their amazing variety, their beautifully contrived shapes and fascinating habits. And I am captivated by the spirit of them. I find in them a longing to communicate and a real capacity for love. If sometimes they do not trust but fear man, it is because he has treated them with arrogance and insensitivity.

Toward the end of the 1920's I undertook extensive remodeling of my house in San Salvador. With the amount of time I now spent there, and with the number of friends who came to stay with me—like Horszowski, Maurice Eisenberg, and Sir Donald Francis Tovey—I needed more space. Then, too, comfortable as the house was, it lacked certain facilities—there was, for example, scant room for my books and the mementos I had accumulated over the years. I added on several rooms. One was a large music room, capable of seating several hundred people for concerts. Adjoining it

I built a room I called *Salle de Sentiments.* Here I hung pictures of my mother and father, the Count de Morphy, my teachers and close friends, and here I kept certain cherished souvenirs, such as the windowsill stone I'd been given in Vienna from the room in which Beethoven had been born. Another room was one I had had transported intact from the eighteenth-century palace of a Catalan nobleman named Count de Guell. For me it embodied Catalan culture. It was a lovely salon with wall panels of paintings depicting allegorical and pastoral scenes, a magnificently decorated ceiling, and graceful crystal chandeliers. Fronting the house I erected a high sea wall with a walk on top—you had a spectacular view of the ocean from there. About the grounds I added gardens, terraces and pools, which were shaded by cypress trees and provided the setting for several marble statues I had commissioned.

My favorite statue was one of Apollo. When I had first told the well-known Catalan sculptor, José Clará, that I wanted him to make an Apollo for me, he had been incredulous. "A statue of Apollo?" he said, laughing. "For modern sculptors, that's a thing of the past."

"No, don't laugh," I told him. "As I conceive of Apollo, he is not simply one of the ancient gods. For me he epitomizes the noblest qualities of man. You are a gifted sculptor, and you can make me an Apollo."

He shrugged. "All right, Maestro . . . if that's what you want . . ." He was not exactly enthusiastic.

Sometime later I returned to Clará's studio to see how his work on the figure was progressing. He had made two maquettes. "Those are lovely studies of athletic youths," I told him, "but they are not Apollo." He was obviously skeptical. The next time I visited him, I brought along a book of mythology. I read him some passages about Apollo. I could tell from the way he listened that he was getting interested.

Casals' villa and estate at San Salvador, Spain

"You see," I said, "there is nothing dated about Apollo. He remains many things in one. He is not only the god of music and poetry who enchanted other gods with his playing of the lyre. He is also the god of medicine—the ancients understood the affinity between music and medicine, the healing qualities of both. You perhaps think of Apollo as an athlete because he was the patron of sports—but how much more he is! He deified the human form. He is an archer whose arrows are not used for war but against evil monsters. He brought harmony both to celestial bodies and to the affairs of men. And think of his concern for the simplest people, for sailors, travelers, emigrants—as the guardian of wayfarers, he watches over them and blesses them with gentle winds, safe harbors and new homes . . ."

Clará sat for some minutes in silence. "All right," he said, "I shall try again."

He did. He kept working until finally he produced the Apollo that I longed to have. It is in my garden still at San Salvador—and despite the grief and turmoil of the intervening years, the ideals it embodies for me have not changed.

And when recently, for the first time since man came on this earth, he reached beyond it and voyaged toward the stars, how fitting it was that his ship should be named after Apollo—protector of wanderers and symbol of man!

It was in the winter of 1931 that my beloved mother died at the age of seventy-seven. I was away from San Salvador on a concert tour in Switzerland at the time—where I had been, strangely enough, at the time of my father's death twenty-five years before. And again, as when my father died and I had a premonition of it, an extraordinary thing happened.

I had a dear friend in Florence whose name was Alberto

Passigli. He was a prominent Italian businessman who was also an outstanding patron of music, and we had known each other intimately for years. On the day I received the telegram telling me of my mother's death, Passigli arrived in Geneva, where I was performing. He had come from Florence, he said, because he had felt I faced some sort of crisis and needed him. He did not know, of course, that my mother was dying, but his compulsion to come to me had been so great that he had simply left his business affairs and come to Geneva to be with me. . . .

I have said what my mother meant to me, and though I knew she would one day have to die, it was somehow impossible for me to think of the world without her. I mourn her to this day. She was buried beside my father in the little graveyard near the church in Vendrell.

A Portfolio
of
Contemporary
Photographs

by Albert E. Kahn

"For the past eighty years I have started each day in the same manner. . . . I go to the piano, and I play preludes and fugues of Bach. . . . It is a sort of benediction on the house."

"Of course, I continue to play and to practice. I think I would do so if I lived for another hundred years."

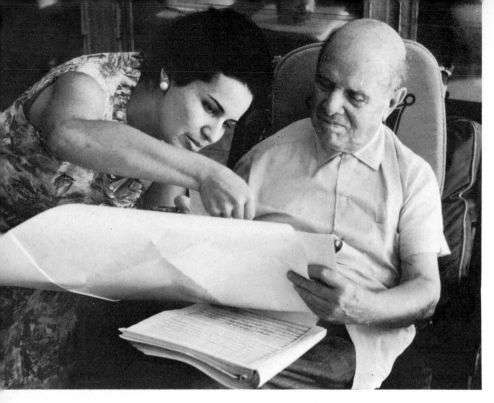

"Martita is the marvel of my world, and each day I find some new wonder in her."

"One of my recent students has been that fine young cellist, Leslie Parnas."

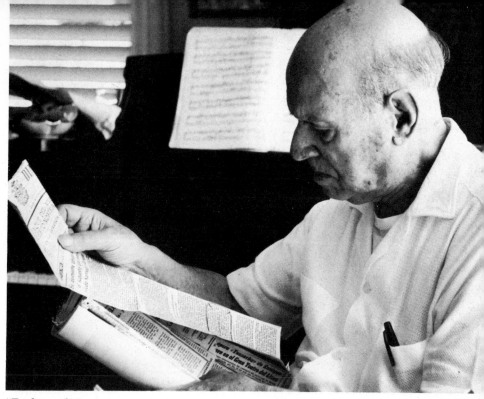

"Each week I receive from Barcelona a package full of clippings from different magazines and newspapers."

"My friend, Alfredo Matilla, who was associated with the Spanish Republican Government, is now a professor at the University of Puerto Rico and an official of the Festival Casals."

"Each time we come together for the first rehearsal of the Festival Casals at San Juan, it is like the reunion of a family. : . . My friend, Sasha Schneider, who has done so much to make the festival possible is always there. . . ."

"Sometimes during intermissions at the concert performances I feel exhausted, and it is an effort to restore myself."

"Only recently I was listening to one of Sarasate's old records, made
at the turn of the century. . . .
"What an extraordinary virtuoso he was!"

"The Wild West was still a reality in the days of my first visit to America—when I now watch cowboy programs on television, I'm reminded of the western towns where we gave concerts on that tour."

"It was early in 1962 that I decided to take my peace oratorio, *El Pessebre*, anywhere in the world I could and conduct it as a personal message in the cause of international understanding and world peace. . . . I am a man first, an artist second. As a man, my first obligation is to the welfare of my fellow men."

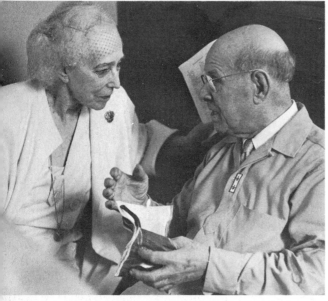

"In 1960 I accepted an invitation from my dear friend, Rudolf Serkin, to conduct master classes at the summer music festival at Marlboro, Vermont. Since then I have not missed a single summer. . . . My old friend, Queen Elisabeth of Belgium, attended the festival in 1962. At Marlboro, I find a special joy."

"The last Prades Festival I attended occurred in the summer of 1966. . . . Many dear friends came. . . . I had some wonderful music sessions in my cottage with the Soviet violinist, David Oistrakh, the American pianist, Julius Katchen, and my old friend from Switzerland, the cellist Rudolf von Tobel. . . . One afternoon the Catalan chorus serenaded me by singing my own song, *O Vos Omnes.* . ."

"In the evenings at my home in Puerto Rico the four of us play dominoes together. Rosa is my partner—she plays a splendid game. We keep a running score, and Rosa and I are usually a good many points ahead of Martita and Luis. 'Don't get discouraged,' I tell them. 'You may catch up with us when I'm one hundred.'"

"The Puerto Rican poet, Tomás Blanco, dedicated a poem to Martita and me, and I composed music for the words. When I listen to the recording of that song, I feel my heart is singing—"

See in the waves of the sea
How much I love you.
I love you from the depths
    of my sleeplessness,
For love is the inner memory
    of far away yesterdays. . .

See in the blossoming flower
How much I love you.
I love you from the calm of
    my contentment,
For love is the perfume of my
    present happiness.

I love you beyond space and time.
I love you on this earth.
And now I love you. I love you.

xi
Triumph and Tragedy

If the year 1931 held for me the sorrow of my mother's death, I think of it also as a year of birth. It was in the spring of that year that the Spanish Republic was born.

A few days after the establishment of the new government, I conducted my orchestra at a ceremony celebrating the proclamation of the Republic. The concert took place in the great palace of Montjuich in Barcelona, and seven thousand people were present. We performed Beethoven's Ninth Symphony. At the end of the concert, the President of the newly formed Catalan government, Francesc Maciá, declared the Republic had come into being on the wings of the Hymn to Brotherhood—that noble chorale with which the Ninth concludes.

I was then fifty-three years old. I had conducted Beethoven's Ninth many times. But that spring night the glorious words of the Finale had a symbolic significance for me that they had never had before.—

> *O friends, friends, no more of those sad tones!*
> *Instead, let us all raise our voices*
> *In a joyful song! . . .*
>
> *Praise to Joy, daughter of Elysium,*
> *Born of God!*

Goddess, merging love and laughter,
To thy shrine we come!
By this magic is united
What the harsh past held apart.
All mankind are sworn brothers
Where the gentle wings abide!

For me, at that moment, there was a true joining of man
and music. For me that moment symbolized what the people
of my country had dreamed of throughout long years of
struggle and suffering—the coming into being of a government dedicated to the highest aspirations of man, to freedom and happiness and universal fraternity. That moment
was a triumph for the people of all Spain—for the people
of all nations. Alas, who then foresaw that this triumph
would end in terrible tragedy?

The first years of the Spanish Republic—the years up
until the outbreak of the Civil War—were among the most
meaningful years of my life. I am not a politician. I have
never belonged to any political party. I see much that is ugly
in politics. But an artist with a conscience cannot separate
himself from certain political issues. Chief among those
issues are justice and freedom. And it was the Republican
government that brought justice and freedom to Spain.

From childhood I was taught by my parents to venerate
the ideals of the Republic, and since youth I had known that
my place was with the people. What man who loves humanity can feel otherwise? The great majority of the people
of Spain wanted a true democracy—this was shown at the
elections when the people voted overwhelmingly for the
Republican government. For too long they had endured
hunger and illiteracy; they had chafed for generations under
the arrogance and corruption of the army, the aristocracy,
and other such institutions. They wanted justice and a de-

cent way of life. Like most artists and intellectuals in
Spain, I was with them in these aspirations. Then, too, as a
Catalan, I felt a special gratitude to the Republic for granting
Catalonia the autonomy that my compatriots and I had
longed for over the years. Yes, for me the birth of the
Spanish Republic represented a culmination of my dearest
dreams.

At the time of its founding, there were those who said
the Republic was a Communist regime. This of course was
nonsense. It was a myth cultivated, and perhaps even believed, by that minority who opposed the Republic's popular reforms—by the sort of people who are always opposed
to democracy. It was propaganda spread by the fascists—
by Franco and by Hitler and Mussolini, who later used it as
an excuse for intervening in Spain. Some well-meaning persons, I know, were fooled by this propaganda—people can
sometimes be made to believe very foolish things. Actually,
most of the reforms the Republic brought to Spain had
existed for decades in other European countries. You might
say the Republic represented a New Deal for Spain, corresponding perhaps in some ways to Roosevelt's New Deal
in the United States. For grandees obsessed with the idea
of keeping their feudal privileges and power, all of this no
doubt seemed revolutionary in the extreme. But the fact was
that when the Spanish Republican government and the
Generalitat of Catalonia were formed, there was not a single
Communist in either government.

The government leaders during the days of the Republic
were no ordinary politicians. They were in fact extraordinary personalities, men of the best quality and highest
culture—scholars, scientists, university professors, poets—
men of social conscience and lofty ideals. I do not believe
that there had ever been before any government made up
of such a group of savants and humanists. I think of men

like Manuel Azaña, and Dr. Juan Negrín, two of the prime ministers of the Republic. A gentle and brilliant man of letters, Azaña was a fine essayist, a novelist, and Spain's foremost translator of Voltaire and other foreign authors; Dr. Negrín was a world-renowned physiologist, a professor at the University of Madrid—his erudition was legendary. I think of Fernando de los Ríos, the Minister of Education, a philosopher and linguist; the journalist and author Álvarez del Vayo, who became Foreign Minister; and the noted Catalan historian, Nicolaú d'Olwer, who was another Cabinet member. These eminent men—and other government leaders like them—were so dedicated that during periods of special repression and martial law under the monarchy, some of them had served prison terms—and even faced death sentences!—rather than abandon their ideals.

The government leader for whom I had perhaps the greatest respect and admiration was the first Catalan President, Francesc Maciá. He was a true patriot, a man of great courage and dignity, who was imbued with the history and noble traditions of Catalonia. He had quit a military career —he had been a lieutenant colonel in the Spanish army— in order to devote his life to the cause of Catalan independence. Some said he was quixotic, but he never gave up. He was hounded and persecuted by the police, imprisoned for his political activities, and forced to live for years in exile. The Catalan people adored him, and in towns and villages throughout Catalonia he was called *el avi*—"the grandfather"—he was more than a father to the people, he was their grandfather! I had never voted in any election in Spain before 1931; I did not care for the sort of candidates who ran for office under the monarchy. But when I heard Maciá speak, I said to myself, This is the man for me; and the first political vote I cast in my life was for him. He was a handsome man with large mustaches, and though he was seventy or so when we first met, he still carried himself like a soldier. I had occasion to see him often while he was President—we had wonderful conversations. And how courteous he was to me! He would never pass through a doorway before me. When he died in the winter of 1933, the whole nation grieved.

One of my dearest friends in the Catalan government was the poet Ventura Gassol. For some years he had been an intimate colleague of Maciá—though he was young enough to be Maciá's son. He became Minister of Culture in the Generalitat. Gassol was a small, highly sensitive and passionately patriotic man, who always wore a long bow tie. His company was a pure delight. By profession he was a teacher, and he had a wonderful way with children. He had great musical understanding. His taste in music was perfect —it was instinctive with him.

One incident tells much about Gassol. Between Vendrell and Barcelona there is a stretch of road which rises steeply over quite a distance. Whenever I traveled along it, I used to think of the time when there had been no cars or trucks to carry vegetables, fruits and other supplies to Barcelona, and all of this transportation had been done with carts drawn by horses and mules. I would picture in my mind those poor beasts struggling up that grade, with their drivers shouting at them and beating them, and I would think of their weariness and pain and with what effort they had performed their task. At the top there was a sort of café where the drivers had stopped for something to eat and to water their horses. One day I described that scene to Gassol. "What would you think," I said, "of erecting a monument there to those animals who brought such riches to the city of Barcelona and who suffered so much to do it?" Gassol— being the poet he was and visualizing the whole thing— exclaimed, "What a thought! What a wonderful idea! We will do it." There was no hesitation in him at all. He decided, just like that, and immediately gave orders for plans to be drawn up for the monument. Unfortunately it was never built. The Civil War put an end to that project, as to so many plans and hopes. . . .

Under the leadership of men like Maciá, Gassol, Azaña and the others, a veritable cultural renaissance took place in Spain. It was inspiring to see—yes, and more inspiring to be part of it! When I was offered political posts, I said no, that it was against my principles to hold any political office. But I then was asked to become president of the Junta de Música—the Council of Music, a division of the Cultural Council of Catalonia. I readily agreed. We used to meet once a week for three hours at the Generalitat, and almost always Gassol attended our meetings. The purpose of our work was to plan and organize all manner of cultural endeavors in Catalonia.

Since boyhood I had cherished the arts, and through the Count de Morphy I had come to understand the true meaning of education—now I saw art and education made available to all the people, not just to the well-to-do but to the poor people in the cities and peasants in the villages alike. The idea I had fought to achieve through my own orchestra and through the Workingmen's Concert Association—the idea of bringing music to the common people—was now put into practice in all phases of culture from one end of the country to the other. The rate of school construction was ten times as rapid as it had been under the monarchy. During the first years of the Republic, almost ten thousand new schools were built! And many of them in the rural areas, where illiteracy was widespread. In the schools of Catalonia it had been forbidden under the monarchy to teach the Catalan language; only Castilian was taught. What is more shameful than denying a child the right to learn his native tongue and destroying his pride in the culture of his own people? All of that was changed under the Republic. Children were now taught Catalan in the schools. They learned Castilian too but first Catalan. They were also taught the history of their land, with its great scholars and heroes, and the richness of their cultural heritage. The Catalan flag now flew in Catalonia, alongside the flag of the Republic.

One phase of the Republic's vast program of education was especially exciting to me. It was supervised by the Institución Libre de Enseñanza—Free Institution of Education. This organization had been originally founded in the late 1800's by a group of college professors—led by the great art critic, Manuel Cossío—who had been expelled from their teaching posts for refusing to take an oath of loyalty to "Crown, Church and Dynasty." The organization's hope was to bring learning to the backward, isolated villages of Spain. Under the Republic, college professors and students began carrying out this program on a major scale, taking classics of the theater into the most remote regions, and helping the villagers build schools and libraries, with books that they themselves supplied.

In those remarkable days artists and teachers—all those who brought culture to the people—were treated with special consideration by the government authorities. I myself was shown the utmost solicitude. During my lifetime I have been awarded honors by different governments, and they have shown much thoughtfulness to me—in fact, I have often felt I did not deserve the recognition I received. But never, at any time, have I been treated with such tenderness and love, with such embracing concern, as by the Catalan Generalitat and the Spanish Republican government. There was nothing they would not do for me and my music; they did not overlook the smallest detail in facilitating my work. This was true not only of government officials but also of municipal authorities, trade unions, university faculties. I was showered with honors—to the point where I was embarrassed and said, "Please don't do these things. There has been too much." In some cities, streets were named after me—like the beautiful, leafy Avingunda Pau Casals in Barcelona; there were public celebrations and civic tributes to me in many towns. I was declared an adopted son of the city of Barcelona and made an honorary citizen of Madrid. I remember especially the concert I gave on that occasion in Madrid. The ovation afterwards was overwhelming; it seemed the audience would never leave—they applauded and applauded. Then, gradually, they left in small groups—and the last to remain applauding, sitting in his box until the very end, was the prime minister, Manuel Azaña!

I recount these honors not because of vanity but because of what they indicate of the Republic's attitude toward culture. I was profoundly moved by them at the time because I knew they were a manifestation of the people's love —and for me this is the highest honor of all.

Under the monarchy I had been treated with great affection by the royal family. But I cannot say this warmth of feeling was always reflected in the conduct of government officials. On my concert tours in those days, for example, no representative of the Spanish monarchy—ambassador or consul—ever met me at the station when I arrived in some foreign city for a performance. But when I went abroad during the days of the Republic, if I visited a city with a Spanish embassy or consulate, I would invariably find the ambassador or consul waiting for me at the station, and he would put a car at my disposal and do everything possible to be of help to me during my stay. I do not mean I was treated like some visiting dignitary. Just the contrary. I was made to feel like a member of the family.

Actually, I was so busy with affairs in Catalonia that I was less inclined than in the past to travel abroad, but there was one trip I was especially glad to make. That was to Scotland in the autumn of 1934. It was on that trip that I met Albert Schweitzer for the first time. We had been invited to receive honorary doctorates at the University of Edinburgh. My old friend, Sir Donald Francis Tovey, was then professor of music at the university; he had also invited me to conduct the Reid Symphony Orchestra in Edinburgh in the first performance of a cello concerto he had composed and dedicated to me—he himself had founded and was conductor of that splendid orchestra. Besides being probably the greatest musicologist of our time—I have never known anyone with his knowledge of music—Tovey was a wonderful composer. He was also a superlative pianist, in some ways the best I have ever heard. The fact is I regard Tovey as one of the greatest musicians of all time.

I had looked forward eagerly to meeting Schweitzer. Not only was I familiar with his writings on Bach, but I had of course an intense admiration for him as a man. On that occasion in Edinburgh there were a number of public and private concerts, and Schweitzer became very excited over my playing of Bach. He urged me to stay on—he wanted to hear more Bach—but I couldn't stay, because of other engagements. I had to catch a train after my last performance, and I had gotten my things together and was hurrying down a corridor when I heard the sound of running footsteps behind me. I looked around. It was Schweitzer. He was all out of breath. He looked at me with that wonderful expression of his which mirrored the great compassion of the man. "If you must leave," he said, "then let us at least say goodbye with intimacy." He was speaking in French. "Let us *tutoyer* one another before we separate." We embraced and parted.

From that day on, we remained in close touch. Great distances separated us—Schweitzer was of course in Lambaréné most of the time—and we were able to meet only two other times. But we frequently wrote to one another, and in the years following the Second World War we joined forces in our efforts to halt atomic bomb tests and warn people of the dire menace of nuclear war.

What a giant of a human being he was! He was truly the conscience of the world. Even in our bitter times it is enough to think of him to have hope for humanity.

The leaders of the Spanish Republic knew there were matters on which I differed with them—I never hesitated to express these differences. They knew that though I was a republican, I remained devoted to members of the Spanish royal family. But they respected my sentiments. On one occasion, a few years after the establishment of the Republic, there was an evening of tribute to me at the City Hall of Madrid. A great crowd attended. Among those present were top government officials. It was a wonderful, festive affair, and—as is always the case on such occasions—there were many speeches. The mayor of Barcelona delivered the main address. At the end of the celebration I was asked to *tomar la palabra*—to "take up the word." I do not like to make speeches, but I was so touched by the things that had been said that I wanted to convey what was in my heart. I spoke of my childhood in Vendrell and of the early days of my musical career. I told about my student days in Madrid, and about my neighbors in the garret where my mother and I lived—the shoemaker, the cigar makers, and the porter who worked at the palace. Then I spoke of the time I spent at the palace and of my deep continuing affection for Alfonso. "For whatever I am, for whatever I have accomplished as a musician," I said, "I owe more than I can ever put into words to that wonderful woman, Queen María Cristina. She was like a second mother to me and I shall always think of her with love." My words were halted by applause. The whole audience rose to its feet. Yes, the government officials—men who had devoted their lives to fighting against the monarchy and for the Republic—they too arose and applauded. And why? Because these were people of magnanimous hearts and they accepted me for what I was. When they applauded, I wept. I wept because of their love and understanding, and because I was proud to be one with them. . . .

The Spanish Republic came into being at the time of the greatest economic crisis the world had ever witnessed—and the early years of the Republic were those of the Great Depression. Unemployment, hunger and despair were widespread in the world. Disaster hovered over many lands. In Germany the people turned in desperation to Nazism, and the dark cloud of fascism began to spread across Europe. But in Spain the popular mood was one of elation and hope. I do not mean that the Republic was a panacea and that the government did not make mistakes—it made many. What government does not? And some of the intellectuals who held office in the Republic were perhaps more idealistic than practical—personally, I have always attached more value to principle than to practicality. But whatever problems there were, the march was forward. And the people of Spain knew it.

There were elements, however, who had a different feeling. They were the same reactionary elements who had opposed the Republic from the beginning—they fiercely resented the democratic reforms and the diminishment of their privileges. They conspired against the Republic and sought to exploit its every weakness. For a time, in 1934, these elements regained some political power. They used it ruthlessly. On the advice of Generals Manuel Goded and Francisco Franco, the army brought in Moorish troops and Foreign Legionnaires to use against striking miners in the Asturias and massacred many of them. When the Spanish people voted again for the Republic in new elections, the intrigues of the reactionaries and fascists intensified. There were acts of provocation, violence, killings—plots and intrigues. Sometimes one felt the country was a seething volcano.

In the summer of 1936 the volcano erupted. I was in Barcelona at the time preparing to conduct a concert. By strange coincidence, it was scheduled to take place in the very hall at the palace of Montjuich where—a little more than five years before—I had conducted Beethoven's Ninth Symphony to celebrate the proclamation of the Republic. And again I was to conduct a performance of the Ninth—this time at a government ceremony entitled "Celebration for the Peace of the World." The final rehearsal took place at the Orfeó Català on the evening of July 18. I shall never, never forget that day. In the morning word came over the radio from Madrid that there had been a military uprising in Morocco—an uprising staged by fascist generals who were reported to be planning a nationwide insurrection in Spain and the overthrow of the Republican government. All day tension had mounted in Barcelona and rumors ran wild. Some people said that revolts of army garrisons under fascist officers were already under way in a number of cities. Nobody knew what the situation really was. By nightfall the avenues and plazas were thronged with people —with soldiers, Civil Guards, factory workers in overalls, and crowds of agitated men and women. Everybody's radio was on. Over loudspeakers set up in the streets, messages were being broadcast by the government: *"Do not turn your radios off! Stay calm! Traitors are spreading wild*

*rumors to sow fear and panic! Keep tuned in! The Republic
is in control of the situation!"*

I made my way through the seething streets to the Orfeó
Català for the rehearsal. We had completed the first three
movements and were about to begin the Finale—I had just
called the chorus onto the stage to sing the chorale—when
a man rushed into the hall. He handed me an envelope, saying breathlessly, "This is from Minister Gassol. An uprising is expected at any moment in the city." I read Gassol's
message. It said our rehearsal should be discontinued immediately . . . all the musicians should go straight home . . .
the concert scheduled for the following day was to be
canceled.

The messenger told me that since the message had been
written, an insurrection had started in Madrid and fascist
troops were now marching on Barcelona.

I read the message aloud to the orchestra and the chorus.
Then I said, "Dear friends, I do not know when we shall
meet again. As a farewell to one another, shall we play the
Finale?"

They shouted, "Yes, let us finish it!"

The orchestra played and the chorus sang as never before
. . . *"All mankind are sworn brothers where thy gentle
wings abide!"* I could not see the notes because of my tears.

At the end I told my dear friends, who were like a family
to me, "The day will come when our country is once more
at peace. On that day we shall play the Ninth Symphony
again."

Then they put their instruments in their cases, and we all
left the hall and went out into the street, where the people
were setting up barricades.

The fascist uprising in Barcelona was crushed in one day.
It was crushed not only by troops loyal to the Republic but

also by the working people of the city. Most of these Catalan workers were unarmed. While gunfire swept the streets, they stood beside soldiers and picked up the weapons of those who fell. In some places, barehanded, they stormed and took fascist strongholds bristling with machine guns. Workers riding in trucks drove right into buildings, smashing in the doors. The plazas and streets were strewn with dead and wounded. But by nightfall the government forces were in complete control of the city; and the fascist commander, General Goded—he had landed that morning by hydroplane in the harbor to lead the revolt in Barcelona —had been captured with all of his staff. The Catalan president, Luis Companys, persuaded the general to speak over the radio. Goded told his followers that he had fallen prisoner and that further fighting was useless.

Next morning we learned by Radio Madrid that the uprising in Madrid and many other cities had also been defeated. In some regions, it was said, the fascists had temporarily seized power, and General Franco was reported to have landed in Spain with Foreign Legionnaires and Moorish troops from Morocco. But most people felt that the general insurrection had failed, and that within a short time the Republic would regain control throughout the country. We did not then know, of course, that Nazi Germany and Fascist Italy would soon start pouring guns, tanks and planes, and tens of thousands of troops, into Spain to aid Franco. Nor could we imagine that the Republic—the legal, democratically elected government of Spain —would be denied the right to receive arms by the Nonintervention Agreement. . . .

All war is terrible but civil war is most terrible of all. Then it is neighbor against neighbor, brother against brother, son against father. And that was the nature of the war that was to rack my beloved country for the next two and a half years. They were a nightmare of unrelieved horror.

The splendid achievements of the Republic were drowned in blood. The nation's finest young men perished—yes, and countless women and children. Hundreds of thousands were driven into exile. There are no scales in which to measure such human suffering.

In the weeks following the suppression of the uprising in Barcelona, an appalling situation developed. Though the revolt had been crushed, the violence was by no means ended. Many people were outraged by the rebellion and maddened by the deaths of their fellow citizens. Now they sought vengeance and took the law into their own hands. There were elements—particularly among the anarchists, whose movement was very strong—which ran wild. They summarily executed not only known enemies of the Republic but people they suspected of fascist sympathies. They burned churches and opened prisons. Criminals and gangs of young ruffians roamed the cities and countryside pillaging and robbing. There was a breakdown of constituted authority. A period of chaos ensued.

I was horrified by these developments. I went to the Generalitat and urged the strongest measures to halt them. "What is happening is intolerable," I said. "These are dreadful crimes, dreadful injustices. Countless innocent people are suffering. In the countryside around Vendrell, for example, the anarchists and others are now seizing all cars. Sick people have no way of getting medical care. You must send soldiers and restore order."

I was told, "We are doing everything we can, but the situation is partly out of control."

"You are destroying the good name of the Republic," I said. "If you have lost control, you should resign from the government."

They said, "In that event, there would be no government in Catalonia. . . ."

I went to the headquarters of the anarchists. What

strange men they were! They listened to me respectfully, but I felt they did not understand what I was saying. They believed their actions were entirely justified. Many of them were philosophical anarchists. They were opposed to authority and had no respect for the law. "The people are the only law," they told me. In some ways, strangely enough, these men seemed to me like children.

One day two armed men burst into the room in which I was practicing the cello in my home at San Salvador. "We have come to arrest Señor Rennon!" they said. "We were told he is here." Señor Rennon was a Barcelona businessman who owned a nearby summer residence. I told the men he was not in my house. They left. Soon they returned. They had my neighbor with them. His wife stood there weeping. They told me, "We want to use your telephone to call Vendrell and have them send a cart." I knew what that meant—they probably intended to execute my neighbor. I said, "If anyone uses the phone, it will be me, not you. You are not taking this man anywhere." They glowered at me, and for a moment I did not know what they would do. Then they seemed to get a little uncomfortable and they said they were acting on orders from the mayor of Vendrell. I telephoned the mayor. He knew from my tone how angry I was. He said, "Oh, those men must have made a mistake. I instructed them to go to another place." I told the men what the mayor had said. They would now go from my house, I said, and leave my neighbor with me. They were obviously furious. But they went. . . . That incident illustrates how "justice" was often meted out in those days!

Such things were happening not only in Catalonia. There was a breakdown of authority in other parts of the country. Government spokesmen, trade union leaders and prominent persons broadcast appeals to the people urging them not to take the law in their own hands and to respect the authorities. But it was weeks before the government really regained control of the situation.

In every war, of course, outrages are committed on both sides—what, indeed, is a greater outrage than war itself? But one thing must be said about the Spanish Civil War. Those outrages which occurred in territory held by the Republican government were not the product of government policy—they were the acts of irresponsible and uncontrollable elements which took advantage of the chaotic situation. The government deplored these outrages and took measures to halt them.

But with the fascists it was entirely different. The fascist leaders did not seek to halt outrages but in fact encouraged vicious repressions and persecutions in territory under their control. With them, terror was an instrument of official policy. They planned and practiced terror systematically not only through ghastly, organized mass executions in Burgos, Badajoz, Seville and other cities under their military juntas, but also through constant savage bombing of Barcelona, Madrid and other civilian centers in Republican territory. Those frightful bombings, in which thousands upon thousands of innocent men, women and children died, were often carried out by German and Italian planes. The raids —which Picasso symbolized in his famous painting *Guernica*—were the first of that sort in history; they were the forerunner of the bombings with which the world would become tragically familiar in the Second World War. They were an expression of the Nazi policy of *Schrecklichkeit*. . . .

I am no historian, no statesman. I am a musician. But one decisive question—one simple fact—about the Spanish Civil War was eminently clear to me at the time. The responsibility for the war rested with those who sought to overthrow by force a legitimate government elected by popular vote, and who—when they failed at first in that plot—summoned the aid of Hitler and Mussolini. That question, I think, is no longer debated very much. When the Axis launched the Second World War, they did much to clarify the meaning of the Spanish Civil War. But I must say I was not confused about its meaning. I believed then, as I do now, that it is the votes of the people—not the bullets of military conspirators—which should decide what government should exist. For me it was a matter of principle to support the Spanish Republic. How in conscience could I do otherwise?

The only weapons I have ever had are my cello and my conductor's baton. And during the Civil War I used them as best I could to support the cause in which I believed— the cause of freedom and democracy. I became honorary chairman of the Musicians' Committee to Aid Spanish Democracy—the Committee, which was formed in the United States, included among its members such persons as Serge Koussevitzky, Albert Einstein, Virgil Thomson, Efrem Zimbalist, and Olin Downes. I traveled widely—in Europe, South America, Japan—giving benefit concerts to raise funds for food, clothing and medical supplies. I did not go abroad with an easy heart—I felt my place was at home with my countrymen in their dreadful ordeal. Gassol and others insisted I could be of greater help abroad. Sometimes I thought they were trying to protect me—I argued with them but they convinced me of the logic of what they said. I went from foreign city to foreign city with a choking pain inside me. I would read in the newspapers about the battles ravaging my land, the burning towns, the hungry children in cities under siege. While I was playing, I knew the bombs were falling. I could not sleep at night. Often when I spoke with people, I felt as if someone else were talking and I was not there. After concerts I would walk the streets, alone, in torment. . . .

Periodically I returned to Spain, and each time I saw more frightful evidence of the havoc and agony of the war. Great areas of Barcelona were in ruin. Skeletons of buildings on every side. The city overflowed with refugees. Food was desperately short. I gave concerts—in hospitals, theaters, institutions for homeless children. The situation among the children was worst of all—it was unbearable to see. Thousands were homeless and orphaned; thousands had been killed and wounded in the endless air raids. In Barcelona alone there were hundreds of mass bombings. On one occasion, for three days in a row without letup, the fascist planes bombed the city at regular intervals of three hours. And the people of Barcelona at that time had not a single plane with which to defend themselves! And no real air-raid shelters—nowhere to hide from the bombs!

Once, in the middle of a rehearsal I was conducting at the Liceu, bombs started falling nearby. The whole building shook, and the musicians scattered in the hall—as was not unnatural. I picked up a cello on the stage and began to play a Bach suite. The musicians returned to their places, and we continued the rehearsal. . . .

The miracle was the spirit of the people. Not only the heroism of the soldiers who were fighting against immense odds but the heroism of ordinary men and women in every block of the city. With what courage and dignity they went about their work! It was an epic. . . . The words No pasarán! were on everybody's lips. Everyone knew the motto "We would rather die on our feet than live on our knees." What a contrast between those words and the notorious toast of General Astray, the fascist founder of the Spanish Foreign Legion, "Long live death!"

Two episodes I personally experienced summed up the essential differences between the Franco forces and those of the government of the Republic.

The first episode concerns General Queipo de Llano, who was one of Franco's aides and a chief propagandist for the fascists—he was, one might say, their Dr. Goebbels. He was a revolting man, a degenerate. During the war he gave frequent broadcasts from Seville, where he was in command. His broadcasts, which were often directed toward the people in Republican territory, were full of vulgarity and crude, ugly stories—a barracks-room type of humor. Also, he would make threats about what the Moorish troops under Franco would do to women who supported the Republican government—that was the sort of man he was!

One night I heard Queipo de Llano speak about me. He said, "That Pablo Casals! I will tell you what I will do to him if I catch him. I will put an end to his agitation. I will cut off his arms—both of them—at the elbow!" And when he said this, his aides—a clique of them often sat around him as he broadcast—all of them burst into laughter. The fact that this story relates to me is incidental. It demonstrates the mentality of the fascists, their attitude toward culture—and especially their inhumanity. It was the same attitude as that of the Nazis, of Hermann Göring who said, "When I hear the word 'culture,' I reach for my revolver!"

The second episode, which concerns the Republican government, happened during a most crucial period of the war—in the autumn of 1938, when the situation was growing increasingly desperate for the Loyalists. One day Gassol asked me if I would perform at a special concert for the Children's Aid Society, which would be broadcast. I said yes, of course, I would. But I did not know at first what the government was planning. They announced on the radio and in the newspapers that I was to play and also that during the two hours of the concert all work was to stop in the territory of the Republic! The workers in the factories would put down their tools, the activities would stop in government offices—everything would halt, so that all the people might listen to the music! For me that concert had a profound significance. It demonstrated how men and women, fighting for their very lives, at a moment of gravest crisis, found time to express their love of art and beauty. It was an affirmation of the indomitable spirit of man.

The concert took place at the Liceu on the afternoon of October 17. The hall was filled to overflowing, and the audience included many soldiers—many of them wounded, and many on stretchers. The entire government Cabinet, including President Azaña and Prime Minister Negrín, and high army officers were present. I played two concertos— one by Haydn and the other by Dvořák. During the intermission I delivered over the radio a message addressed to the democratic nations of the world. I gave it in English and in French. I said: "Do not commit the crime of letting the Spanish Republic be murdered. If you allow Hitler to win in Spain, you will be the next victims of his madness. The war will spread to all Europe, to the whole world. Come to the aid of our people!"

Alas, that message went unheeded. The Chamberlain Government was still in office in England—they had just concluded the Munich Pact with Hitler and did not wish to offend him. The great majority of the British and French people desired to aid the Spanish Republic, but the Non-intervention Agreement continued to deny us arms. Thousands of American young men formed an Abraham Lincoln Brigade and came to join the International Brigade and fight for democracy in Spain; but the Republic could buy no military supplies from the United States—despite President Roosevelt's sympathy—because of the embargo on arms to Spain. Years later I read that Roosevelt told his Cabinet at the end of the war that the embargo was a grave mistake. . . . The only countries from which the Republic could buy arms were Mexico and Russia, and these supplies were inadequate to meet the huge amount of aid in men and materiel that Hitler and Mussolini continued to send Franco. And so the war moved inevitably toward its tragic denouement. . . .

I am sometimes asked what I think would have happened if the Western democracies had come to the aid of the Spanish Republic and whether this might have prevented the Second World War. One cannot of course rewrite history, but it is clear that Hitler might have been stopped before the frightful catastrophe of that war. We know he should have been stopped when he was taking over one country after another in Europe. Certainly Spain proved to be the last chance. And one thing history will surely record. It was the Spanish people who first took up arms in defense of democracy against Hitler and fascism. The sacrifices and heroism of the Spanish people set an example for the world. Lovers of freedom must never forget those men and women who fought that lonely terrible fight in Spain. Not a day passes without my thinking of them. Those dear noble friends, living and dead—they are with me always. . . .

Toward the end of the Civil War one of the most extraordinary events of my life occurred. The fall of Barcelona was expected at almost any moment. Franco's troops were massing for an all-out attack, and the city was under constant bombardment by Italian planes. Evacuation had already begun in some areas. Such were the circumstances under which I received a message from officials of the University of Barcelona notifying me that before they disbanded they wanted to confer on me an honorary doctorate as their final official act! I was hurriedly escorted to the university. The faculty members—many who had wives and children to be evacuated—had gathered to attend the ceremony of my receiving the diploma. There had been no time to have the document printed—it was lettered by hand. Could any man find words to acknowledge such an honor?

It was a few days later that I bade goodbye to my brothers and their families in San Salvador and departed from my homeland for France. That was more than thirty years ago. Since then I have lived in exile.

xii

Exile

How often in this century of wars and revolutions has the world witnessed the tragic flight of people from their homelands! Each exodus has been a saga of human suffering, and none has occurred under more ghastly circumstances than the flight of the anti-fascist refugees from Spain in the early days of 1939. More than half a million fugitives made their way across the Pyrenees in the dead of winter—men, women and children struggling over the mountain passes in the dreadful cold. All the way from Barcelona the roads were massed with refugees. Some were in cars, trucks and carts. Tens of thousands trudged along on foot, carrying a pitiful handful of belongings. Many of the sick and aged died in that procession of sorrow. At night, in the freezing rain and snow, the people slept in the streets of villages or in fields beside the highways. Again and again, as they fled toward the French border, they were strafed and bombed by fascist planes.

And in that exodus were the best and noblest people of Spain—the soldiers and poets, workers and university professors, jurists and peasants who had championed freedom and would not bow to tyranny.

One might have thought that when those brave tormented souls reached France, they would have been treated with honor and compassion. Such, alas, was not the case. The Daladier government—the same politicians who had recently come to terms with Hitler at Munich—felt little sympathy toward the anti-fascist refugees. They granted asylum to the Spanish Republicans only with reluctance and because of public pressure. I learned what was happening at the border from horrified compatriots who came to see me in Paris. "Our people are being put in concentration camps under armed guards," they told me. "They are being treated as if they were enemies or criminals." I could hardly believe such a thing was possible. But soon I was to see those camps with my own eyes. . . .

When I had arrived in Paris toward the end of the Civil War, my dear friends Maurice and Paula Eisenberg had insisted I stay with them. They showed me loving care—all the warmth of their gentle hearts. But no amount of solicitude could heal the anguish in me. I was overwhelmed by the disaster that had befallen my homeland. I knew of Franco's reprisals in Barcelona and other cities. I knew that thousands of men and women were being imprisoned or executed. Tyrants and brutes had turned my beloved country into a monstrous prison. I did not know at first what had happened to my brothers and their families—word reached me that fascist troops had occupied my home at San Salvador. These things were too horrible to think about, but I could not drive them from my mind. They surged up in me—I felt I would drown in them. I shut myself up in a room with all the blinds drawn and sat staring into the dark. Perhaps in the darkness I hoped to find forgetfulness, relief from the pain. But an endless panorama passed before my eyes—horrors I had witnessed in the war, scenes from my childhood, faces of dear ones, cities in ruin and weeping women and children. I remained in that room for days, unable to move. I could not bear to see or speak with anyone.

I was perhaps near to madness or to death. I did not really want to live.

Finally the Eisenbergs persuaded me to see an old friend, Guarro, from Barcelona. Later he told me how shocked he was when he saw me—he hardly recognized me. He talked to me for hours. "You cannot stay any longer here in Paris," he said. "You must leave immediately." He urged that I go to a little village in the south of France near the Spanish border—in French Catalonia. Its name was Prades. "Many of the people there, you know, speak our language," he said. "You will think you are in Catalonia." I said it was no use, but he insisted. "You will be close to your countrymen in the refugee camps near there. They need your help—they need help terribly." In the end I agreed to go.

So it was that in the spring of 1939 I came to Prades. I could not have imagined at the time that I would spend the next seventeen years of my life in this little town in the Pyrenees. And in spite of the sorrow in me, I found respite in my surroundings. With its winding cobbled streets and whitewashed houses with red tiled roofs—and the acacia trees that were then in bloom—Prades might have been one of the Catalan villages I had known since childhood. The countryside seemed no less familiar to me. The lovely patterns of orchards and vineyards, the wild and craggy mountains with ancient Roman fortresses and medieval monasteries clinging to their sides—these too were a replica of parts of my homeland. Indeed, centuries before, this very region had been part of the nation of Catalonia.

I took a room at the one hotel in Prades. It was called the Grand Hotel. Its accommodations were perhaps not regal, but the view from the window of my little room was surely fit for a king. Close by, Mount Canigou rose toward the heavens. This magnificent mountain—which is celebrated in the works of our beloved Catalan poet, Jacinto Verdaguer

—has a special meaning for Catalans. Perched in solitary grandeur on one of its crests is the Abbey of St. Martin, which was built at the beginning of the eleventh century by Count Guifred. According to legend, this count's great-grandfather—the founder of the Catalan dynasty—created the flag of Catalonia, with its four stripes on a yellow background. Mortally wounded in battle, he dipped his fingers in his blood and drew them down the face of his shield, declaring, "This shall be our flag."

Shortly after arriving at Prades, I visited some of the concentration camps—there were a number nearby, at Rivesaltes, Vernet, Le Boulou, Septfonds, Argelès—where the Spanish refugees were confined. The scenes I witnessed might have been from Dante's *Inferno*. Tens of thousands of men and women and children were herded together like animals, penned in by barbed wire, housed—if one can call it that—in tents and crumbling shacks. There were no sanitation facilities or provisions for medical care. There was little water and barely enough food to keep the inmates from starvation. The camp at Argelès was typical. Here more than a hundred thousand refugees had been massed in open areas among sand dunes along the seashore. Though it was winter, they had been provided with no shelter whatsoever—many had burrowed holes in the wet sand to protect themselves from the pelting rains and bitter winds. The driftwood they gathered for fires to warm themselves was soon exhausted. Scores had perished from exposure, hunger and disease. At the time of my arrival the hospitals at Perpignan still overflowed with the sick and dying.

When I saw the frightful conditions in those camps, I knew I had but one duty. With several friends who, like me, were fortunate enough to have their freedom, I immediately set about organizing aid for the refugees. My room at the Grand Hotel became our office. We began sending out letters—I myself wrote hundreds of them—to organizations and individuals in France, England, the United States and other countries, describing the tragic plight of the refugees and asking for help of any sort. The response was wonderful. Gifts of food, clothing, medical supplies and money poured into Prades. We worked without letup, day and night, carrying on the endless correspondence, loading boxes of supplies onto trucks which took them to the camps. Sometimes I accompanied the trucks to the camps to help in the distribution of the supplies. Of course there was never enough—so many were in desperate need!

I visited the camps as often as I could. Each time I dreaded going, because of the suffering I would see, and afterwards I could not sleep at night. But I knew how the inmates longed to see and talk with a fellow countryman from the outside. I started corresponding with many of the refugees —especially with those in camps too far away for me to visit regularly. I would spend hours each day writing letters and cards, seeking somehow to relieve their suffering by sending them funds and giving them a word of encouragement. My efforts, Heaven knows, were pitifully inadequate. But how grateful those people were! And with what courage and dignity they bore their lot!

After a while I was joined in this work by Joan Alavedra, the Catalan poet, whom I had known well in Barcelona. He was a man of great energy and diversified talents. During the days of the Republic he had been an aide to President Companys, and at the end of the war he had escaped across the border with his wife and two children. He was well acquainted with the conditions at the camps—this gifted artist had himself been in one of them for weeks before managing to secure his release. Now he took a room adjoining mine at the Grand Hotel, and we became inseparable

companions. He was especially concerned about my health
—I was suffering from severe headaches and dizzy spells.
He said I was trying to do too much. Of course that was
impossible—indeed, how well off I was in comparison with
those in the camps! He gave me a walking stick so that I
could knock on the wall to his room in the event I needed
aid during the night.

Occasionally, to supplement the funds for refugee relief,
I would give benefit concerts in Paris and other cities in
France. I received numerous invitations to play in other
countries, but I could not accept them. There was too much
to do in Prades, and I never stayed away for more than a
couple of days at a time. Moreover, quite often I found it
difficult to play. I was doing so much letter writing that my
hands had a tendency to tremble.

That September, less than six months after the end of
the Spanish Civil War, the catastrophe occurred that I had
anticipated with dread—which I had warned would happen
if Hitler were not stopped in Spain. Hitler invaded Poland
and unleashed the Second World War.

I was besieged with letters from musicians and other
friends in England and the United States urging me to leave
France and to make my home in their countries. I was
deeply moved by their concern for my welfare and the wonderful opportunities they proposed for the continuation of
my musical work. I recall one offer from the United States
for something like a quarter of a million dollars for a series
of concerts! But I knew that now more than ever my place
was in France. Here my career had started and the doors of
the world had been opened to me; here were many of my
oldest and dearest ties. How, then, could I leave this country
—which was, one might say, my second home—in the hour
of her travail? Even more decisive was my duty to my com-

patriots in the concentration camps. I continued to work with the refugees and to give occasional benefit concerts.

In the summer of 1940 the war took a disastrous turn which confronted me with a new and crucial situation. Hitler's armies suddenly turned west. In less than a month they swept through Holland and Belgium and penetrated deep into France. The Allied forces were retreating on all fronts. French resistance seemed to be falling apart, and there was talk of treachery in high places. One day, early in June, we received word that the Germans were nearing the outskirts of Paris—the fall of the French capital and the surrender of France were at hand. It was also reported that Franco was about to declare war on France at any moment, cross the Pyrenees, and occupy French Catalonia.

Alavedra and I decided we must leave Prades—to remain, it appeared, meant falling into the hands of the Nazis or the Spanish fascists. We were told we might be able to secure passage on a boat, the *Champlain,* which was due to sail for America any day from Bordeaux. But how to reach Bordeaux? The city was over two hundred miles away, and all public transportation was at a virtual standstill. Alavedra managed to find two taxi drivers who were willing to make the trip. We burned all the correspondence in our files—some of it, we feared, might compromise anti-fascist refugees and lead to their arrest if Hitler's or Franco's troops came to Prades. Then we hastily threw together a few of our belongings, and, with Alavedra's wife and children and several friends, we left in the two taxis.

In Bordeaux we found utter chaos. Thousands of people milled about the city—many of them had fled southward from the Germans and were seeking to escape the country. The streets were full of trucks, carts and cars loaded with furniture and other personal belongings. Everywhere were scenes of the wildest confusion. Rumors ran wild. Some people said that Nazi panzer divisions were approaching, others that the city would soon be bombed. Alavedra set about the task of securing passports for our group—I was too ill to be of help. He learned my old friend and colleague, Alfred Cortot, was in the city and went to see him. Cortot, he knew, had influential connections with the French authorities, and Alavedra hoped to enlist his assistance in our behalf. But Cortot said there was nothing he could do. When Alavedra told him how sick I was, he simply said, "Give him my regards and tell him that I wish him well." He did not come to see me. I could not understand his conduct at the time, but before long, when Cortot became an open collaborationist with the Nazis, I was to realize with sorrow why he had acted this way toward me. It is terrible, the things that some people will do because of fear or ambition. . . .

Somehow Alavedra managed to arrange for our passports and tickets on the *Champlain*. Then, when we were preparing to go to the place where the boat was due to dock, we heard the news—German planes had bombed and sunk the *Champlain!*

We did not know what to do. We were all famished and exhausted. But it was impossible to find hotel rooms or any other quarters in Bordeaux—one could not even get food at the cafés. Our only course, we decided, was to return to Prades. We started back in our taxis. The return trip seemed interminable. The roads were clogged with troops and refugees. We crawled along—it took us two days to get back. The first night we slept in the taxis. Finally, around midnight on the second day, we reached Prades.

When we drove up in front of the Grand Hotel, we found that the doors were padlocked. Alavedra pounded on them. The owner of the hotel appeared in a window. When Alavedra told him why we'd had to return, the proprietor said

our rooms had been taken. Alavedra asked if we couldn't
have beds for the night. He told the man that I was ill.

"The Germans may arrive at any time," the proprietor
said. "And what if they find I've given shelter to Casals?
Everyone knows he's an enemy of the Nazis. I have my
family to think of."

Meanwhile a man who owned a nearby tobacco shop had
been awakened by the noise. He offered to put us up for
the night. "You will have to forgive me," he said. "I do not
have any extra beds. But at least you will have a roof over
your heads."

And so we slept on the floor at his house.

People have been very generous to me over the years and
given me many gifts. But I can think of none that remains
more precious to me than that night's lodging in the humble
home of the tobacconist.

Next day we found temporary quarters in an apartment
in Prades, and shortly afterwards we managed to rent a
house on the outskirts of the town. It was a small two-story
house set back from the road among lovely old gardens and
trees. Alavedra and his family occupied the first floor. I
moved into a room under the eaves—with my cello and a
somewhat antiquated piano I had acquired. The house was
called Villa Colette. It was to be my home for the next
decade.

With the surrender of France and the establishment of
the Vichy regime under the aging Marshal Pétain, our situation at Prades became increasingly precarious. Although
the south of France was still unoccupied by the Nazis, fascist sympathizers and collaborationists assumed authority
everywhere. Once again I sought to do what I could to help
the Spanish refugees in the concentration camps—I gave
benefit recitals for them in Perpignan, Marseilles and other

towns. But it was constantly more difficult to help them. The plight of the refugees was even worse than before—many were compelled to work in so-called labor battalions, which were little more than a form of organized slavery. As the months went by, the atmosphere around me grew more and more strained. Some of the townspeople became openly hostile. Others, with whom I had been friendly, turned away when they passed me on the street. I knew what pressures they were under and that they feared any association with me might lead to their persecution by the fascists. But those were bitter days. At times I felt old and isolated from the world.

And, indeed, there were apparently those in the outside world who felt isolated from me—or, at least, had no idea what had happened to me. Later I learned that a report was published in the United States to the effect that I'd been shipped back to Spain and was languishing in a dungeon at Montjuich, awaiting execution! Yes, things can always be worse than they actually are. I understand that my friend Maurice Eisenberg, who by then had emigrated to America, wrote a letter to *The New York Times* denying the rumor and saying I was still free and giving occasional benefit recitals for the refugees.

Of course not all of life was bleak. I think that perhaps it never is—even under the worst of circumstances. A few friends among the residents in Prades still came to see me surreptitiously, and their visits were heart-warming. Also, I had the companionship of Alavedra and our little circle at the Villa Colette. And there were other Catalans who were free and with whom I kept in touch. One of them was my old and dear friend, the poet Ventura Gassol—the former minister of culture in the Catalan government during the days of the Republic. On one occasion, in fact, our continuing comradeship resulted in some trouble for both of us!

It seemed that as long as Gassol and I had been friends we stimulated each other so much that when we got together we often came up with some exciting idea. And one day such an idea occurred to us in Prades. A few miles from the town, at the foot of Mount Canigou, was the ancient Abbey of Saint-Michel de Cuxa—it had been founded as a Catalan monastery in the ninth century and had become an artistic and religious center in the Middle Ages. In later centuries the deserted abbey had fallen into a state of disrepair. During the time of the Spanish Republic, citizens of the Catalan town of Ripoll had sent a wonderful bell to be installed in one of its towers. What a fine idea it would be, Gassol and I agreed, if we now went to the abbey and rang that bell as a patriotic gesture to show our fellow countrymen that the spirit of Catalan patriotism was still alive! And so we went and rang the bell. It was an unforgettable moment—there, in the serenity of those old pillars and arches, and the shadowed cloister with its worn flagstones—when the rich sounds of the bell pealed forth to the surrounding mountainsides! But the Vichy authorities did not appreciate that moment as much as we did. When they learned from local residents what we'd done, there was a scandal. The newspaper in Perpignan featured an article on its front page denouncing Gassol and me as Reds, anarchists—yes, and even assassins! Actually, of course, we were none of these things. We were just a Catalan poet and a Catalan musician.

The only regular sources of news available to us in those days were Vichy propaganda organs like that newspaper in Perpignan. It was highly depressing to read them—as it was to listen to the Vichy-controlled radio broadcasts. But we had another, unofficial source of news, which never failed to sustain our spirits and buoy our hopes even in the harshest times. That was the British Broadcasting Corporation. How we savored every fragment of news on those nightly broadcasts from London! It was from the BBC that we learned in 1941 of the entry of Russia and the United States into the war against the Axis—then we knew it was only a matter of time before the fascist forces of darkness would be crushed. It was over the BBC that we heard the inspiring news the following year of the mounting military efforts of the Allies, the devastating defeat of the Nazis at Stalingrad, and the great victory of the Anglo-American forces in North Africa. With what jubilation we learned of those victories!

Our rejoicing, however, was tempered by developments that swiftly ensued. That winter, to protect himself against the expected Allied landing on the Continent, Hitler occupied the whole of southern France. German troops were stationed in Prades. For the first time I lived among men who wore the hated swastika. From the moment Hitler had come to power in Germany I had refused to play in that country —that birthplace of Beethoven and Bach which had been so dear to me—but now the Nazis had come to me. We were virtual prisoners of the Germans.

If the situation had been difficult before, it now became almost intolerable. Both Alavedra and I were placed under the constant surveillance of the Nazis. We were known to them as foes of fascism. Moreover, the French partisans of the Maquis who began operating in the area were joined by Spanish refugees who had escaped from the concentration camps, or secretly crossed the Pyrenees, and we were suspected of being in touch with them. Periodically the Gestapo came to search our house. I could never fathom what they expected to find. But then of course one cannot unriddle the workings of minds such as theirs. Anyway, they let me know that if ever they did find whatever they were looking for, things would go hard with me. Both Alavedra's name and mine, I was informed by a Frenchman who posed as a friend of the Nazis, headed one of their lists of suspects for possible arrest or execution as hostages.

I constantly expected to be arrested. But perhaps the Nazis feared such an action might arouse too much clamor. They knew I had many friends in various countries. Shortly after the Nazi occupation of Prades, for example, a group of eminent musicians in the United States—including Toscanini, Ormandy and others—had petitioned the German government to let me leave France and grant me safe-conduct to Portugal. And I suppose that even in Nazi Germany there were some influential personages who still considered themselves lovers of music.

Even though I remained free—in the sense of only being under what amounted to house arrest—my existence became literally a struggle to survive. Food had been scarce enough before, but under the Nazis rationing became far more drastic. They parceled out supplies to their favorites among the population and were ready to see the rest starve. At the Villa Colette we existed for the most part on a fare of boiled turnips, beans and other greens. Milk or meat was an unheard-of luxury. When we found a potato or two, it was cause for celebration. When we fell sick, there were no medicines. Another problem, in the winter, was the cold. We had no coal and little wood. Every day I would go out and, limping along with the aid of my cane, gather sticks and branches that had fallen from the trees. I wore my overcoat indoors and out. I have always suffered from the cold, and now rheumatism began to plague me. Playing the cello became increasingly difficult for me, though I continued to practice. I felt exhausted and ill most of the time.

Then, in the summer of 1943, something happened which I think in retrospect did much to help sustain me during the remainder of the war. I began the composition of my oratorio, *El Pessebre*, "The Manger." No doubt there was in me at the time the need to work on some undertaking of this sort. Yet the work on the oratorio began, as such things often do, in an almost accidental way.

One day Alavedra and I learned from friends of ours that a Catalan Language and Poetry Festival was being arranged in Perpignan. Prizes were to be awarded for original writings in the Catalan tongue. Without telling me, Alavedra submitted a poem he had brought with him in a notebook when he fled across the Pyrenees from Spain. It was a long poem he had written several years before in Barcelona for his five-year-old daughter, Macía. He had, in fact, written it at her request—as a song for them to sing together on Christmas Eve beside the miniature manger they had built together.

At the Festival in Perpignan, Alavedra's poem was awarded first prize. When I heard it recited there, I was so impressed with its beauty—it was so simple and yet so profound, as is the tale of the Nativity itself—that I made up my mind to put the words of the poem to music. I did not let Alavedra know my intention. The day after the Festival, working secretly in my room, I began composing the music. The following month, on the occasion of Alavedra's saint's day in June—that of St. John—after embracing him and wishing him a happy birthday, I said I had a surprise gift for him. I led him to the piano and played the first fragment of my composition, while singing the words from his poem. Then I told him of my plan to set the whole poem to music. . . .

For the next two years I worked steadily on the composition. It was not always easy to maintain my schedule of work—there were distracting events and sometimes I was too hungry and weary to concentrate properly on the music. But each day, in the morning when I was freshest and after I had played my Bach at the piano, I endeavored to compose for a certain number of hours. In spite of our privations, and the doubts and sorrows that afflicted us, the work nourished my spirit. In the midst of the savagery of war I was writing music about the Prince of Peace, and if the suffering of man was part of that tale, it also spoke of a time when man's long ordeal would be ended and happiness would be his at last.

When Christmas came, my friends and I would hold a little ceremony based on that part of the oratorio I had finished. We would gather in my room around the piano and sing the songs of Joseph and the fishermen, the laborer and the plowman, and the choruses of the three Wise Men and the angels. Our voices would join in that sorrowful question in the choruses of the camels and the shepherds:

> *How steep are the mountains*
> *We must cross. . . .*
> *How long must we travel*
> *Through foreign lands*
> *Feeling so weary?*

One morning I was in my room working on *El Pessebre* when I heard a car pull up in front of the house. I looked out of the window. Three German officers were approaching. They knocked on the front door, and I heard them ask if I was in. I was afraid my friends might try to conceal the fact that I was, and this might get them into difficulty. I called downstairs, "Send them up." As I heard the footsteps on the stairs, I thought that perhaps this was the moment I had feared. . . .

When the officers came into my room, they clicked their heels and gave the Hitler salute. Two of them were quite young and one was middle-aged—they wore immaculate uniforms and gleaming boots. They were large well-fed men, and they seemed to fill my little room. To my surprise, their manner was courteous, even respectful.

They said, "We have come to pay our respects. We are great admirers of your music—we have heard about Casals from our parents, about concerts of yours they attended. We want to know if you are comfortable and have everything you need. Perhaps you could use more coal, or perhaps more food."

I said no, that my friends and I had everything we needed. I wondered what they were driving at.

They looked around my room curiously. One of them— he was the oldest one and obviously the leader—asked, "Why do you remain in such cramped and shabby quarters? Why don't you return to Spain?"

I said, "I am against Franco and what he represents. If there were freedom in Spain, I would go. But if I went now, I would have to say what I believe. People in Spain who say what they believe are put in prison or worse."

"But surely you can't want to live in this Godforsaken town where there's not even anyone to hear your music."

"I am here because it is my choice."

Soon they got to the point. They said, "You know, you are loved in Germany. Everybody knows about your music. And we have come to extend an invitation to you from our government. You are invited to come to Germany and play for the German people."

I said, "I am afraid I cannot go."

"And why not?"

"Because I have the same attitude about going to Germany that I have about going to Spain."

There was a strained silence. They exchanged glances, and I sensed they were restraining themselves with difficulty.

Then their leader said, "You have the wrong idea about

Germany. Der Führer is greatly interested in the arts and in the welfare of artists. He loves music especially. If you come to Berlin, he himself will attend your performance. You will be welcomed by all the people. And we are authorized to say that a special railroad car will be placed at your disposal. . . ."

For a moment these men seemed not menacing but ridiculous. There was something so crude—so childish—about the idea that a private railroad car might influence my decision! I said, "No, my going would not be possible under any circumstances. You see, I have been suffering from rheumatism lately, and my giving any concerts is out of the question at this time."

After a while they gave up trying to persuade me.

Their leader then asked if I would give them an autographed photograph. I gathered they wanted it to show their superiors they had been there, and I complied with his request.

"And while we are here," he added, "perhaps you would do us a personal favor. Would you play some Brahms or Bach for us?" I had the strange feeling that this Nazi officer actually wanted to hear me play.

I told him that the rheumatism in my shoulder wouldn't permit my playing.

He walked to the piano, sat down and played a passage from a Bach aria. When he had finished, he said, "May we see your cello?"

I took my cello from its case and placed it on my bed.

They stared at it. "And is this the instrument on which you played in Germany?"

I said that it was.

One of them picked it up, and the others touched it. And suddenly I felt deathly ill. . . .

Finally they left me. But when they got to their car, they didn't drive away. They sat there for several minutes, got out and started back toward the house. I stepped onto my porch to find out what they wanted. They asked me to remain standing where I was, and they took several photographs. I suppose they wanted them as additional proof of their visit. After that, they drove away.

Following the Allied landing in Normandy in the summer of 1944, the tension in Prades mounted daily. The Maquis intensified their guerrilla activities in the surrounding countryside, and the Germans retaliated furiously with harsh measures against anyone they suspected of aiding the partisans. Hardly a day passed without word of new arrests and hostages being shot. One day a young man who was engaged to the daughter of friends of mine came to see me surreptitiously. He was a member of the Vichy militia— he was only seventeen and had joined the militia to avoid being sent to Germany for forced labor. He was terribly agitated.

His militia chief, the young man told me, had informed him that any day there might be a roundup of persons in Prades. The chief had said that I was among those to be arrested. "We'll give that Casals a lesson," the chief had said. "We'll show him what it means to be against us."

The young man had been courageous enough to speak out in my behalf. "Casals is a musician, not a politician," he told his chief. "If you harm him, people will never forget." He believed his protest had had some effect but he could not be sure. He begged me to go into hiding if possible.

I thanked him for his warning and did my best to calm him down.

Soon afterwards matters reached a climax. The Nazis— in one of their bestial reprisals—burned a nearby village and shot many of the inhabitants. A few nights later a band of Maquis stormed into Prades and attacked the Gestapo headquarters. They killed two officers and wounded a number of soldiers. Now everyone was sure the Nazis would take savage measures in Prades. Terror spread through the town. People kept off the streets. Alavedra and I expected to be arrested hourly.

And then an extraordinary thing happened—it was one of those unpredictable events that sometimes determine the fate of people. The mayor of Prades, a retired military man, went to see the German general in Perpignan who was in command of the whole area. He told the general he wished to assume personal responsibility for the raid at Prades and that he had come to surrender himself. The general was apparently impressed by his conduct. To everybody's astonishment, the mayor was not arrested—and no action whatsoever was taken against the people of Prades! A few months later, when the Germans evacuated the town, this same mayor was arrested as a collaborator and given a lengthy prison term. Such are the whims of war!

The young militiaman who had intervened in my behalf was also arrested on charges of being a collaborator after the liberation of Prades. When I learned he was to be tried, I wrote the president of the tribunal, stating that I wished to testify in his defense. I was summoned to the proceedings at Perpignan. Three other young men were being tried with him on the charge of collaboration. I sat with them on the same bench in the courtroom. How dreadful it was to know these young men were all possibly facing death! And that was the sentence three of them received—yes, three of them were shot. Only the young man for whom I testified was spared. He was sentenced to thirty years' imprisonment. He was set free after several years, and he came to see me. "I owe my life to you," he said. I told him that probably I had only settled a debt, that probably I owed my life to him.

And so two lives were saved—two lives amid tens of millions lost! How much solace was there in that thought?

xiii

Return to Prades

I had lived with war for a long time—almost ten years had passed since the outbreak of the Civil War in Spain—and when peace came to Europe, it seemed at first almost like a dream. There was of course widespread jubilation in France. The people were intoxicated with the air of victory and freedom. And what a change took place overnight in my situation! Nobody, it seemed, could do enough for me. My days were filled with interviews, receptions, offers of degrees from various institutions, lavish banquets. Sometimes at those banquets I used to think what I would have given a few months before for just one of the rolls of bread now left half-eaten on the tables! I moved among crowds of well-wishers, and Catalan flags flew everywhere I went. The French government awarded me the Cross of a Grand Officer of the Legion of Honor. I was made an honorary citizen of a number of French towns. One of those towns was Perpignan—I was greeted there with headlines in the very same paper that had formerly branded me a villain and assassin when I rang the bell at the Abbey of Saint-Michel de Cuxa!

But deeply as I appreciated these generous attentions and manifestations of affection, my mind was preoccupied with other matters. My exiled compatriots released from the con-

Letter from Georges Bidault, President of the postwar Provisional Government of France, to Albert Sarraut, former president of the Conseil. The letter reads: "Mr. President, You have very much wanted to convey to me your personal support of the promotion of Maître Pablo Casals to the rank of Grand Officer of the Legion of Honor. This artist, I know, combines magnanimity of heart and strength of character with musical genius. He is one of the consciences of our time and I take pleasure in telling you that I have readily signed his order of promotion. Please accept, Mr. President, the assurances of my high esteem. Bidault"

centration camps or returning from slave labor in Germany were in desperate need. Few had any means of subsistence. Many were sick, crippled, half starved. And thousands of French people too were in dire circumstances, homeless and destitute. There was much to be done! I gave benefit concerts for Spanish refugee relief, for the Red Cross and other such causes. I visited the homes that had been established in some towns for Spanish orphans. Each of those little figures represented a tragedy. Looking into their sorrowful eyes, who could take comfort in his own fortunate lot? My mind was haunted too by thoughts of the crowded prisons in my own land. Millions had fought and died for the victory that had been won over fascism. Now, above all, I longed to see my people liberated from fascist tyranny. . . .

In June of 1945 I was invited to visit England. A whole epoch seemed to have gone by since I was last in that dear land. One can imagine how I looked forward to seeing my old friends! When I went to buy my ticket at the office of the British Airways in France, I was told, "What—you expect to pay? Why, that's impossible! You are our guest!" At the London Airport when I submitted my baggage for customs inspection, the officials smiled and shook their heads. They would not touch my things.

I had of course known of the terrible Nazi air raids on London, but I was sickened by the havoc I now saw—the gutted remnants of buildings, the great craters and piles of rubble, whole blocks obliterated. All were ghastly reminders of the bombings I had witnessed in Barcelona. But again, here in England, I found proof among the ruins that no amount of bombing can erase the spirit of man. From talking with Englishmen, one would never have guessed the ordeal they had survived—they simply did not mention their sacrifices and suffering. In fact, they seemed to radiate optimism and good cheer. And this, one knew, was not only because they had won a great victory but because nothing could defeat people like this.

In an interview with the *London Philharmonic News,* I addressed a message of respect and love to the British people. I related how those of us in Nazi-occupied territory had hung on the words of BBC and how London had been for us the Capital of Freedom. "Today," I said, "it is the Capital of Hope." I spoke of another matter close to my heart— the magnificent role of British musicians during the war. To the members of the London Philharmonic Orchestra, I said:

From my little refuge in the Pyrenees I have watched from hour to hour the experiences through which your great country has passed, and I have accorded no more importance to the actions of your political and military leaders than to the countless achievements of your leading symphony orchestra and soloists. I know how you have traveled under bombardment from town to town to keep alive the cause of great music, and I know, too, how those years of trial have created millions of new listeners to the works of the great masters.

I gave concerts in a number of cities in England. Perhaps the most memorable for me was the concert at the Albert Hall. The last time I had performed with an orchestra was at the Lucerne Festival in the summer of 1939. Then, the conductor had been Sir Adrian Boult; now, six years later, he was again conducting. Thousands packed the hall, and there seemed to be even more outside. I played the Schumann and Elgar concertos, and, as an encore, one of the Bach unaccompanied suites. When I left after the performance, the crowd in the street was so dense that it was some time before the police could extricate my car. I was not impatient—I could have remained for hours among those radiant faces!

One moment stands out from that glorious evening. An elderly man with a white beard and flowing cape was waiting at the stage door after the concert. "Do you recognize me?" he said. It was none other than my old friend, the cellist Agustín Rubio, whom I had first met almost seventy years before when I was a lad of eleven playing at the Café Tost in Barcelona! "Yes," he said, "that night I told Albéniz the time will come when this little one will make a big stir!"

A few days after the concert at the Albert Hall, I was invited to play at the BBC studio and to broadcast a message to my fellow countrymen in Catalonia. When I had finished playing and approached the microphone, I could not at first utter a word—the moment was too much for me. I lit my pipe, and it somehow comforted me and helped me find my voice. "My thoughts fly to you, my dear countrymen, to those in exile and those on our beloved soil," I said. "I have come here from my retreat in the shadow of Mount Canigou, on the other side of the Pyrenees. And first I want to thank my generous-hearted British hosts who showed such heroism in meeting the terrible tests of war and who deserve the gratitude of all who cherish liberty and justice. Now we look to them for the preservation of peace and the moral reconstruction of Europe."

I concluded my message to my compatriots by saying, "I would like to think that when our ancient melody, *El Cant del Ocells*, now reaches you, it will give voice to the love we bear Catalonia. That sentiment, which makes us proud of being her sons and binds us all together, must now make us work as one, as brothers united in a single faith, for a tomorrow of peace when Catalonia will again be Catalonia."

And then I played the "Song of the Birds," the haunting Catalan folk song with which I would conclude all my concert performances from that time on.

Two of Casals' musical treasures: the original page from Beethoven's notebook on which he jotted down his first idea for the opening notes for his Ninth Symphony; and the original score of a Brahms Quartet

One episode after my return to Prades brought back with a sudden shock the darkest days of the war years. I was in my cottage there one morning when there was a knock on the front door. I opened it—and there stood Alfred Cortot.

I felt a terrible pain at the sight of him. The sorrowful past was suddenly with me, as if it all had happened the day before. We stood looking at each other without speaking. I motioned him into my room.

He began speaking haltingly, with his eyes on the floor. He had aged greatly, and he looked very tired. At first he made a half-hearted attempt to excuse what he had done, but I stopped him.

Then he blurted out, "It's true, Pablo. What they say is true. I was a collaborator. I worked with the Germans. I am ashamed, dreadfully ashamed. I have come to ask your forgiveness . . . " He could say no more.

I, too, found it hard to speak. I told him, "I am glad that you tell the truth. Because of that, I forgive you. I give you my hand."

That October I went back to England for another concert tour. The proceeds were to go to a fund for the widows and children of those brave flyers in the Royal Air Force who had died in the war—it was a small enough token of my gratitude to this noble land.

Less than six months had elapsed since the defeat of Germany, and yet, in that brief time, there was already cause for grave apprehensions about the postwar world. The atomic bombs, which in a flash had annihilated hundreds of thousands of human beings at Hiroshima and Nagasaki, cast a shadow over the future of all mankind. What a monstrous irony—that at the very moment of victory over the fascist threat to civilization, man should create a weapon threatening the extermination of the human race!

There were other developments that caused me grave disquiet as I traveled about England that summer. Throughout the dark years of the war I had longed for that day when victory would mean the end of fascism and the liberation of the nations enslaved by it. But now powerful forces seemed to be blocking the full achievement of those goals to which the United Nations were pledged. Though Hitler and Mussolini had been crushed, the fascist dictatorship they had fostered in Spain remained in power. Even more ominous—conciliatory gestures were now being made to the Franco regime. Prominent personages spoke of Franco with deference; newspaper articles praised his so-called accomplishments. Was it conceivable, I asked myself, that the Spanish people—the very people who had first taken up arms against fascism—were to be doomed to continue living under fascist rule? And the hundreds of thousands of refugees who had believed an Allied victory would mean the return of democracy in Spain—including those who had fought alongside the Allies—were they to be condemned to permanent exile? I recoiled at the thought of such a betrayal, but the evidence mounted on every side. Government dignitaries and other influential figures in England sought to reassure me. I must understand, they said, the complexities of diplomacy; I must be patient while matters took their course. Such counsel only served to confirm my worst fears.

I decided that at this crucial time I must act in such a way as to make clear my wholehearted protest against any appeasement of Franco and my complete identification with the plight of my suffering countrymen. Could I continue to be applauded at concerts and to receive awards when my people were in such misery? When I was invited to receive honorary degrees at Oxford and Cambridge universities, I replied that I could not—with the prevailing attitude toward Spain—accept any more such honors. I announced that I was canceling all future engagements in England. My last concert there, I said, would be the one I was scheduled to give in November in Liverpool. I acted with a sorrowful heart, but there could be no compromise under the circumstances.

Some of my friends sought to persuade me to reconsider or at least postpone my decision. That marvelous artist, Dame Myra Hess, with whom I had played several concerts on my British tour, urged that I meet with the secretary to King George VI and arranged an appointment. Our meeting took place at Buckingham Palace. I told the secretary that England and the other members of the United Nations had a clear moral duty to see democracy restored in Spain, and I reminded him of the disastrous role of the Non-intervention Agreement in helping Franco overthrow the Spanish Republic. The secretary listened with respectful attention and assured me he would convey my sentiments to the king. But in my heart I knew it was to no avail.

Back in Paris, I received a wire from Sir Stafford Cripps, who was then prominently associated with the Labour Government, inviting me to meet with him. But by then I was too weary and disillusioned for further discussions. "We would not understand each other," I replied. "We would speak different languages. You would speak about politics, and I would speak about principles."

In France I gave a few more benefit concerts. I still hoped against hope that some of the governments might keep their word to the Spanish people. But, alas, it became ever more clear that their policies toward Spain were now dictated by political expediency instead of the humanistic code of the United Nations. After a short time I announced I would not play again in public until the democracies changed their attitude toward Spain.

I retired to Prades. For the second time, as it were, I went into exile. I cannot say it was an easy thing to do, and I knew that in a world where cynicism widely held sway, my action could hardly affect the course of nations—it was, after all, only the action of a single individual. But how else could I act? One has to live with himself.

If of my own volition I returned in protest to my refuge in Prades and became, you might say, an artist in isolation, I was never really alone in the years that followed. It was not the same as it had been during the German occupation of France. Then I had been entirely cut off from the world. Now I was in close communication with it. True, I had silenced my instrument on the concert stage, but I continued to have not only its companionship but that of dear friends who came to Prades to see me and of friends who wrote to me from other lands. Indeed, many who wrote to me I had never met. Long distances often separated us—yet I felt we reached across the seas and embraced one another.

And what heart-warming support I received from them! An unforgettable demonstration was the occasion of my seventieth birthday in the winter of 1946. On that day messages poured into the little village of Prades from every part of the world—letters, postcards, cables, communications of every sort—from Japan, Palestine, the United States, Czechoslovakia, Africa. Hundreds, thousands of messages! They came from artists and trade unionists, from writers and scholars, from churchmen, Spanish refugees, and former members of the Abraham Lincoln Brigade. Among the greetings from the Soviet Union was a lovely cable signed by Prokofiev, Shostakovich, Khachaturian and other Soviet composers and musicians. In Mexico and other countries, I was told, radio stations played recordings of mine throughout the day.

And in the evening, in my little house in Prades, I heard a concert program on BBC arranged by friends of mine in England. At the beginning of the program Sir Adrian Boult addressed a message to me expressing, as he put it, the greetings of thousands of musicians and music lovers in his country. He spoke about our friendship which had begun more than a quarter of century before when he, as a young man, conducted a concert in Liverpool at which I performed the Schumann concerto, and he told how he'd later come to Barcelona to study my conducting methods. He spoke of my many concerts in England since the turn of the century. He spoke so intimately it was as if he were sitting in my room talking with me. "Maestro," he said, "here we are in the studio with many friends, including fifty cellists. How we wish you were with us! And we hope you will soon visit us again. But we know you are with us in spirit. We are going to play a short program under the direction of your old friend, John Barbirolli. We shall play music that will carry our thoughts to you in Prades."

Then Barbirolli conducted the fifty cellists in the playing of a composition I had written in 1927 for students at the London Violoncello School. It was a sardana, and the music for it had been inspired by the fiestas I had witnessed as a child in Vendrell with the sounds of the *grallas* and the singing of the villagers. . . .

The following day I wrote a letter to *The Times* in which I said:

Ever since my youth when I had the honor of playing before Queen Victoria, I have received many touching proofs of affection from the British public. I count them among the most precious awards of my whole life as an artist. Now, on the occasion of my seventieth birthday, the tokens of affection from all quarters of your country that have reached me in my exile are so numerous that I have to ask the hospitality of The Times *for the expression of my deepest gratitude to all.*

The life of an artist is inseparable from his ideals. I hope that conditions will soon make it possible for me to come and express personally all the affection I feel for the British people.

In the months following my retirement to Prades, I received many communications from England, the United States and other countries, urging me to reconsider my withdrawal from the concert stage. The people who sent these messages had of course the best of intentions, and many said that my music could do more for the causes in which I believed than my silence. From the United States in particular came generous offers, inviting me to give as few or as many concerts as I wished, under any terms I cared to name. I received an especially moving message from a group of eminent intellectuals headed by Albert Einstein urging me to make my home in America. The United States government offered me a special passport. But to all of these communications I replied that, much as I appreciated the spirit that prompted them, I considered it my duty to remain in Prades.

In the summer of 1947 the American violinist, Alexander Schneider, came to visit me for a few days. There was an immediate rapport between us. I was especially taken with his lively humor and passionate enthusiasms—sometimes when he talked his bushy hair seemed to stand on end and I had the feeling his body must have difficulty to keep from flying apart with the energy it contained! Our meeting was to prove the beginning of a precious friendship and one of the most fruitful working relationships of my whole career. Schneider—or Sasha, as his friends call him—is not only a brilliant musician, whose name was linked for years with

the splendid Budapest String Quartet; he is also a remarkable organizer and initiator of musical projects of all sorts,
whose mind teems with ideas. He would, I am sure, have
succeeded in any field of endeavor—in the theater, politics,
business, anything. In one of our first conversations, Sasha
urged me to come and give a series of concerts in the United
States—the fee he proposed was astronomical. I told him,
"But it is not a question of money. It is a purely moral question." And of course he understood.

Some time after he had returned to America, Schneider
sent me a wonderful present from some fellow musicians
and himself. It was a forty-five-volume edition of all of
Bach's works, reproduced from the original Bach-Gesell-
schaft edition, and in it was a touching dedication to me
signed by Toscanini, Koussevitzky, Stokowski, Paul Hinde-
mith, Schnabel, Schneider, Artur Rubinstein and about
fifty other outstanding musicians.

It was not much later that Schneider wrote me that he
had been talking with my old friend Horszowski, and that
Horszowski had made a suggestion about which he, Schneider, was very excited. What Horszowski proposed was that
a Bach festival under my direction be arranged in Prades.
Surely, said Sasha, this would not be inconsistent with my
protest in retiring to Prades. The proceeds, he said, could
go to the hospital at Perpignan, where many Spanish refugees were still being cared for, or to any other such cause I
had in mind. Would I, Sasha wanted to know, be willing to
consider such a festival? With that letter, the idea for the
annual Prades Festivals was born.

At first I hesitated to agree. I wrote Schneider that some
people might misconstrue my taking part in this festival.
Sasha replied, "You cannot continue to condemn your art
to complete silence. If you won't play in public in other
countries, then why not let your fellow musicians come
from other parts of the world and play with you in Prades?

Your protest will remain no less clear." Schneider added that the year 1950 was the bicentenary of Bach's death and that this would be the ideal time for the event. My doubts were resolved, and I agreed to the festival. I was especially gratified by the thought that it would provide me with a means of helping my compatriots, many of whom were still in desperate need.

The Bach Festival took place in June 1950 in Prades. Sasha supervised all of the preparations and also agreed to my request that he act as concertmaster. He arranged for the whole orchestra and for the violinists Joseph Szigeti and Isaac Stern, and the pianists Horszowski, Rudolf Serkin and Eugene Istomin to participate as soloists. The program, which lasted over a period of three weeks, included the six Brandenberg concertos, the six unaccompanied suites for cello, and also violin and clavier concertos. The concerts were held in the fourteenth-century Church of St. Pierre, which faced the village plaza.

What excitement there was in Prades as the opening day of the festival approached! The whole appearance of the village was transformed—the streets were festooned with banners, streamers and posters, and Catalan flags flew everywhere. I have often wondered how it was possible for that tiny town and the neighboring villages to accommodate the fifty musicians who took part in the festival and the hundreds of people who came from all over France and from other countries to attend the concerts. I was told that some had even come from China! "Today," a local shopkeeper said to me, "our village is the music capital of the world!"

Shortly before the first concert, one of the festival officials asked me if I would address a group of Catalans. I thought at first he meant refugees, but no, he told me, they were men and women who had come from Spain.

"But how is that possible?" I said. "I was told the

Hotel Laurelton
147 West 55th Street
New York 19.   N. Y.

February 13th 1952

Beloved Pau

I hope you received a cable from me on your birthday + I want to try + tell you what the experience of Perpignan has done for me. The issues in the world today, are Tremendous + your music is one of the few remaining powers that renew our belief in the ultimate triumph of Truth + Beauty. Everyone who attended your festivals has felt this.

Now you must be patient + hear my own little story. When I left you on that unforgettable Sunday morning in Prades I told you that I would not write to you until my playing had improved. Before every season, I suffer agonies of apprehension + this last Autumn I went through one of the darkest + longest tunnels of despair. It was the memory of your music that brought me back to the light, + now everyone says that something has been added to my playing. I know it has been inspired by your influence.

No words could be adequate + in your great modesty I know you would ask me not to thank you.

The only way I can show my gratitude is to try + understand the revelation of music more + more deeply every time I play.

Ever your deeply devoted
Myra

Extracts from a letter to Casals from Myra Hess, February 13, 1952

Franco government had forbidden Spanish citizens to cross the border to attend the concerts."

"They've come anyway," he said. "They crossed the Pyrenees secretly, on foot."

That group of Catalans included musicians, professors, workingmen—and one bishop! Some were old friends of mine who had been political prisoners in Spain. One of the group was an elderly shepherd from Spain. "I brought my sheep with me over the mountain," he told me.

On the opening night the village plaza was massed with people. The bishop of St. Fleur gave a welcoming speech before the first concert. He requested that there be no applause in the church throughout the performances. And then the festival commenced with my playing Bach's unaccompanied Suite in G Major.

Three weeks later, at the conclusion of the final concert, the bishop of St. Fleur and the bishop of Perpignan arose in the audience and began to applaud. Everyone else in the church stood up and joined in the ovation.

Some time later I received from Japan an album containing the signatures of hundreds of Japanese citizens who had heard recordings of the Bach Festival played in Tokyo. One page was headed "Hiroshima." It was filled with the awkward signatures of young children, boys and girls who were four, five and six years old. And on the page was written this message: "We were born after the dropping of the atom bomb, and already we have learned to love your music." If any doubts about the rightness of my playing at the Bach Festival had lingered in my mind, they would have been dispelled by that message from the children of Japan.

The response to the Bach Festival was so spontaneous— so enthusiastic—that afterwards it was decided to hold an annual music festival in Prades. Schneider again agreed to supervise the arrangements. The second festival was held at Perpignan in the ancient Palace of the Kings of Majorca. It too was an immense success. One thousand people were expected to attend, and almost two thousand came. The festivals of the next two years took place in the ruins of the Abbey of Saint-Michel de Cuxa, the very same abbey where Ventura Gassol and I had rung the bell as a gesture of Catalan patriotism during the days of the German occupation of France—and this time nobody called me an anarchist or assassin for making music at the abbey!

After that, all the festivals were held at Prades in the Church of St. Pierre, where the original Bach Festival had taken place.

The last festival I attended occurred in the summer of 1966. It was shortly before my ninetieth birthday. Many dear friends came from different countries to give me their greetings, and I was deeply moved by their presence.

On the day before the opening of the festival—it was Sunday—two busloads of Catalan workers arrived in the morning from Barcelona. They had come on Sunday because on weekdays they could not get away from their jobs. They left their homes before dawn and drove 150 miles, over the mountains, to Molitg-les-Bains, the village—near Prades—where I was staying. Most of these workers had formerly belonged to the Workingmen's Concert Association which I had founded in Barcelona in 1928—it was banned after the fascists seized power—and some of them were the sons and daughters of former members of the Association. They gathered outside my cottage and gave me flowers. Then, with a small stringed-instrument orchestra they serenaded me with Mozart's *Eine Kleine Nachtmusik*. After that, they left.

Toward the end of the festival another group of my countrymen visited me. These men and women came from my birthplace, Vendrell. Some were members of the choral society which my father had formed there a hundred years before and which exists to this day. The mayor and a priest from Vendrell accompanied the group. In the Catalan tradition of the fiestas I had known so well since childhood, they formed a human pyramid beneath the cottage balcony where I was standing. Perched on one another's shoulders, with the largest men on the bottom, they raised to the top of the pyramid a small boy who was carrying a goatskin wine bag. I took the boy in my arms and drank from the wine bag. I gave him my pipe as a present.

Members of the group—they were wearing the Catalan folk costume of white shirts, red cummerbunds, and red kerchiefs—danced the sardana. And afterward they sang a choral work of mine which I had dedicated to Vendrell.

My heart was so very full—I tried to tell those dear friends what was in it. "People of Vendrell," I said, "I feel that you have come as friends not only to visit me but to invite me to visit you. I have longed to do that ever since the day I left my dear land. But I must tell you that my faith in the people of Catalonia has made me strong enough to resist that longing. I hope that God will grant I live long enough to see again our church's beautiful campanilla whose bells we all love so much, and the guardian angel, and the organ where my father played and I assisted him when I was nine years old. I beg you remember what that means to me and, above all, my love for Vendrell and all of you. Thank you, dear ones, for having come to me."

We all embraced. We wept together both because of sadness and joy. Then they got into their buses and drove back to Catalonia.

xiv

El Pessebre

I have many unforgettable memories of the Prades festivals, but the most wonderful of all is associated with the second festival in 1951. It was at that festival I first met my beloved Martita.

I have cause to thank God for much that has happened in my long life. I have enjoyed much good fortune and much happiness. But the years I have shared with Martita have been the happiest years of my life. I was blessed in my childhood to have a mother like my mother, and I have been blessed in my old age to have a wife like Martita.

I have observed a curious trait in many men—though they do not hesitate to say how much they love their mothers, they are reticent to say how much they love their wives! There is no such reticence in me. Martita is the marvel of my world, and each day I find some new wonder in her. I am aware that I am no longer exactly a youth, but if I speak of her in words perhaps expected of young lovers, it is because that is how I feel about her. Perhaps, indeed, because I have lived longer than most people, I have learned more than most about the meaning of love. . . .

Martita and I first met, as I have said, during the second Prades festival. One day I heard there was a writer who had come from Puerto Rico with his niece—a young cellist—to attend the festival, and he wished to see me. I was told this man, whose name was Rafael Montañez, was a good friend of relatives of my mother—members of the Defillo family who lived in Puerto Rico. I had never been to Puerto Rico. My mother used to speak with great nostalgia of the land of her birth, and I often said to her after I had known some success in my career, "Mother, let me take you there." But she would always reply, "No, later, Pablo. Your work must come first." Sadly, that "later" never came. I had never met any of her relatives, and I was delighted at the opportunity to meet someone who knew them well.

When Martita and her uncle came to my house, I had the impression that for the first time I was touching my mother's homeland. When I looked at Martita, I said to myself, "This is no stranger who comes to visit me." I had the curious feeling she belonged to my family. She was then only fourteen—a lovely child with long black hair reaching down her back—and the thought flashed through my mind that my mother must have looked just like her at that age! Later that resemblance became even more pronounced, and today when I show people my mother's portrait as a young woman they are astonished at how much she and Martita look alike.

It was midafternoon when Martita and her uncle arrived at my house—I had moved from the Villa Colette the year before and was renting a gardener's cottage, which I called *El Cant del Ocells*, on a nearby estate. My schedule was crowded as usual. But there was so much to talk about! More than once Montañez said he thought they had taken up enough of my time and should leave, but I said, "No, please don't go yet." I asked them to stay for supper. It was late in the evening when they left. We had been talking for six or seven hours, but I had not noticed the passage of the time. . . .

After the festival, Martita and her uncle returned to Puerto Rico. I did not see her again for three years. Occasionally I exchanged letters with members of her family. Then, early in 1954, I received a letter from Martita's uncle telling about her progress on the cello. She had, he said, been studying at the Mannes School in New York with Professor Lieff Rosanoff—I had known Rosanoff for years, and he had attended my classes in the early 1900's at L'École Normale de Musique in Paris. Martita's uncle asked if it would be possible for her to come to Prades to study with me. I agreed to accept her as one of my pupils.

Martita and her mother arrived in Prades that summer. A striking change had taken place in Martita—the lovely child of a few years before had become a vivacious young lady. We began her cello lessons. Mrs. Montañez remained for a month or so and then returned home. Martita stayed on at the house of a Catalan family with whom her mother had become acquainted in Prades.

Of all the pupils I have taught, Martita was one of the best. I was impressed from the outset not only by her musical talent but by her remarkable aptitude—I have never had a pupil who learned more rapidly or worked with greater discipline. At the same time, though studying an instrument is of course a serious affair, she brought an irrepressible brightness of spirit to her work. Her gaiety was infectious. I soon discovered she had a wonderful sense of humor. I had never known such a born mimic. Not even Harold Bauer could compare!

Naturally I felt a special responsibility toward her—she was, after all, in a strange land, far from her family and friends—and I wanted her to come to feel at home in Prades. But, to tell the truth, she was a remarkably self-sufficient young woman, and she was soon helping me as much as I helped her! She did all manner of things to facilitate my work. She taught herself Catalan in no time at all—she has a rare facility with languages and today speaks French, Italian, Spanish, English, all with equal ease—and she began assisting me with my correspondence. It was, as it still is, very heavy—I sometimes received thirty letters a day—and I have always considered it a matter of conscience to answer anyone who feels it of sufficient importance to write me. Often, too, Martita would drive me when I went to visit my Spanish refugee friends. We began spending more and more time together. The months went by without my being conscious of the bond that was growing between us. . . .

Then in the late summer of 1955, after Martita had been studying with me for more than a year, I was preparing to go to teach my annual master classes in Zermatt when I suddenly realized how much I dreaded the idea of leaving her. I told her, "You, you will be all alone in Prades! And I will feel alone in Zermatt. I cannot think of going without you." She said she too could not stand the thought of our being separated. She accompanied me to Zermatt and kept notes of my comments during the classes. And that was when I first realized that I had come to love her. . . .

Later we spoke of marriage. I told her, "Please think about it most carefully. I am an old man, and I would not want to do anything to spoil your life. But I love you and I need you. If you also feel this way, would you marry me?" And she said that she could not think of life without me.

That winter, together with Martita, I visited Puerto Rico for the first time. My brother Enrique and his wife María accompanied us.

For me, Puerto Rico was a case of love at first sight! Everything my mother had told me about its beauty I now saw with my own eyes. The brilliant sea, the mountains with their opulent flowers and ferns, the massive cloud formations and luminous fields of sugar cane—they simply took my breath away. Above all, I was captivated by the people, by their dignity and gentleness and warmth. And what hospitality! Everywhere, I was greeted with flowers. One banquet followed another. People hailed me on the street: *"Buenos días,* Don Pablo!" Much of the time I felt I was in Spain. The government provided me with a spacious apartment on the top floor of a tall building overlooking the ocean. One of my greatest ambitions since childhood has been to live in a lighthouse, and this was the closest I ever came to it!

Martita and I visited my mother's birthplace, the town of Mayagüez. And there we discovered an astonishing thing. The house in which my mother had been born in 1856 turned out to be the very same house in which Martita's mother was born some sixty years later! Not only that —but our mothers had both been born on the same day of the same month, November 13! Can one explain that simply as coincidence?

While we were in my mother's house, a number of neighbors, relatives and townspeople gathered in the street outside. I felt that only through music could I say what was in my heart. I went out onto the balcony with my cello, and I played the Catalan lullaby my mother used to sing to me when I was a little child. Then, while I accompanied her, Martita sang some early songs of mine of which my mother had been especially fond. . . .

Soon after my arrival in Puerto Rico, I was invited by Governor Luis Muñoz Marín to meet with him at La Fortaleza. I took an immediate liking to this handsome, expansive man. He reminded me of the scholar-statesmen who had headed the Spanish Republic. He was interested in cultural affairs no less than in politics—he had, in fact, been a poet himself in his youth. We talked about Puerto Rico, and he told me about the impressive program he had initiated to improve living conditions and combat poverty on the island. Now, he said, he was seeking to raise the educational and cultural standards. He wanted to know if I had any suggestions for the musical development of the island. Was it possible, he asked, that I would direct an annual music festival in Puerto Rico like the one in Prades? Then he said impulsively, "Don Pablo, join us and live here! It is the home of your mother. You are already part of our family!"

Others urged me to make my home in Puerto Rico. Martita did not try to influence my decision, but I knew that here she would be among her family and friends. I was especially moved by the thought that I might be of service to my mother's homeland. I began giving serious thought to the possibility of settling on the island.

After several weeks I told Governor Muñoz Marín that I

-->

An exchange of communications between Casals and Albert Schweitzer on the occasions of their eightieth birthdays. Casals' cable to Schweitzer reads: "To you my heartfelt wishes for your magnificent anniversary. Our poor world has need of you, of your word, of your great example—May God protect you—Pablo Casals." Schweitzer's letter to Casals reads: "Dear friend, I learn that you also, you are going to be eighty years old, and that you will be celebrating them in Paris. I would like my congratulations to find you there. Both of us owe a lot to Paris, and we love that city for herself recognizing all that she has given us. How much I would love to be with you in Paris and love to walk with you among the memories she awakens in us. Kept here by hard work, I shall do it in my imagination in the days of October when you will be there. I hope that they will be filled by the October sun, particularly radiant in Paris. It was in October in 1893 that I first came to know Paris. Please greet for me Cortot and Feschotte. I envy their being with you. From the heart your devoted Albert Schweitzer."

Docteur Schweitzer
Lambaréné, Gabon
Afrique Equatoriale

A Toi mes vœux du
cœur pour ton magni-
fique anniversaire.
Notre pauvre monde
a besoin de toi de
Ta parole de ton grand
exemple – Que Dieu
te garde –

Pablo Casals

Albert Schweitzer – Dec. 1956
Lambaréné · Gabon A.E.F.

A Pablo Casals

cher ami. J'apprends que toi aussi tu vas avoir 80 ans et
que tu iras les fêter à Paris. Je voudrais que mes félici-
tations viennent t'y trouver. Les deux nous devons beaucoup à Paris et nous aimons cette ville autant pour
elle-même que par reconnaissance de ce qu'elle nous a
donné. Combien aimerais-je être avec toi à Paris et à me
promener avec toi dans les souvenirs qu'elle éveille en
nous! Retenu ici par le dur travail, je le ferai en
imagination dans les jours d'octobre où tu y seras. J'espère
qu'elles seront ensoleillées par le soleil d'octobre particu-
lièrement radieux à Paris. C'est en octobre que j'ai fait
en 1893 pour la première fois connaissance avec Paris.
Veuille saluer de ma part Contât et Enghotte. Je les envie
d'être avec toi. Je te remercie des aimables lignes que j'ai
reçu de toi dernièrement.

De cœur ton dévoué
albert Schweitzer

was willing to direct a music festival in Puerto Rico. I suggested Alexander Schneider as the ideal man to organize it. Muñoz Marín immediately invited Schneider to come to Puerto Rico to discuss the matter. In a single day the three of us worked out the plan for an annual festival. Sasha agreed to organize it—that of course included assembling an orchestra—and to act as my assistant director. The first festival, we decided, would take place the following spring in San Juan.

In March Martita and I returned to Prades, and that winter, following the Prades festival and my master classes at Zermatt, we moved to Puerto Rico. Muñoz Marín announced that an annual Festival Casals was to be initiated under the auspices of the commonwealth government. The first festival, the governor stated, would take place in the spring of 1957 at the theater of the University of Puerto Rico. There would be twelve concerts in all.

The preparations for the festival were very exciting. A festive air pervaded the island. The building and streets of San Juan were hung with banners and pennants. Electric signs proclaimed WELCOME TO THE CASALS FESTIVAL. . . .

A week before the opening concert, the orchestra musicians arrived from New York with Schneider. Our first rehearsal was scheduled for half past nine the following morning at the University Theater. I arrived about half an hour early. Schneider wanted to introduce me to the musicians right away and commence the rehearsal. But I told him, "No, not until nine thirty. Do you want my friends to get a bad impression of me?"

When the time came to start, I welcomed the musicians and said, "This morning let's not really rehearse. Let's just play to get to know one another." And so we began with Mozart's little A-major symphony. After that, I suggested that we play Schubert's Fifth. I was extremely warm when we began the work—my shirt was wet with perspiration —and as we commenced the Andante movement, I felt an unusual weariness. But the beauty of the music took hold of me. At one point I told the musicians, "You must make an accent here, and it must come from the heart." Then, a few moments later, in the middle of a phrase, a fierce pain gripped my chest and shoulders, and I felt faint. I knew I could not continue. I put down my baton and said, "Thank you, gentlemen. . . ."

I was taken to the dressing room. By then the pain had become intense. I was having a heart attack.

Everyone was so gentle and concerned. I told them how sorry I was to have such a thing happen at such a time— our first rehearsal, and such a wonderful orchestra! The doctors gave me drugs to ease the pain, and I was taken home in an ambulance. I knew I would now be unable to take any part in the festival.

Several thousand people in Puerto Rico and other countries had bought tickets and made arrangements to attend the festival. Many persons had worked night and day preparing for the occasion. Besides, there was so much at stake in terms of the future of music on the island. . . . But there was a marvelous response to the crucial situation. The festival officials called an emergency meeting that same evening—it lasted until four in the morning—and they decided to proceed with the concerts if the musicians were willing. The festival, they said, should be held as a tribute to me! Schneider discussed the proposal with the other musicians. As one man, they agreed to go ahead. They decided not to have any conductor replace me on the podium—Schneider would lead the orchestra from the concertmaster's chair.

And so the festival took place! It was an immense success. Every one of the three thousand seats at the University Theater was occupied on the opening night. The orchestra performed magnificently. "Each man played as if the whole performance depended on him," Sasha told me afterwards. "They played like gods!"

My recuperation was a trying time. I was plagued by the thought that I might never be able to play again—to think of life without work! I had the thoughtful attention of the eminent Puerto Rican heart specialist, Dr. Ramón Suárez, and the care of my own physician, Dr. Passalacqua, and other doctors. Governor Muñoz Marín arranged for the famous heart specialist, Dr. Paul Dudley White, to come from Boston to see me. How considerate and understanding he was! Unless there were complications, he told me, he saw no reason why I should not recover completely and play again. Even so, doubts still afflicted me—if I should recover, how strong would I be? I was, after all, eighty years old. Would I regain full control of my fingers? I chafed at the passage of the weeks. For the first month I was not allowed to move from my bed. I spent another month in a wheelchair, and after that I was allowed to start taking short walks. Finally, without letting the doctors know at first, I began practicing a little each day. It was very frustrating—I felt as if I'd have to learn to play all over again. I had particular difficulty with the fingers of my left hand. But gradually the strength returned. And as I once more found the music of my cello, I marveled more than ever before at that other instrument which made it possible for me to play again. Man has made many machines, complex and cunning, but which of them indeed rivals the working of his heart?

I cannot claim most of the credit for my recovery. All of the time, Martita was at my side. No nurse ever watched over a patient with more loving care—or greater skill! I

am not the only one who says Martita would have made a
remarkable doctor—the doctors themselves say so. Of
course her medicine did not consist only of pills—though
I must say there were plenty of them. Whenever my spirits
lagged, it was she who raised them. She always had something to say to make me laugh when things seemed darkest.
Never for one moment did she seem to doubt that I would
play again. She took charge of all my affairs. She handled
the voluminous correspondence, met with visitors, made
all necessary appointments. Yes, she was everything in one
—dear companion, nurse, manager, secretary, and guardian
angel!

And the fact is that during our married life Martita has
continued to be all these things—and much more. Without
her I could never do my work. In addition, of course, she
makes the loveliness of our home. Indeed, she does so much
that it often troubles me. How, I ask myself, does she find
time for herself?

When I was well on the way to recovery, we decided that
the time had come for us to get married. The ceremony—a
very simple one attended only by a few close relatives—
took place early in August. I was aware at the time that
some people noted a certain discrepancy in our ages—a
bridegroom of course is not usually thirty years older than
his father-in-law. But Martita and I were not too concerned
about what others thought; it was, after all, we who were
getting married—not they. If some had misgivings, I can
only say with joy that our love has deepened in the intervening years. . . .

Shortly after our marriage we moved into a lovely little
house in Santurce, a suburb of San Juan. The house was
right on the ocean—only a few yards separated our back
garden from the water—and all day long the sea breezes
swept through our windows. I had often said that the most

beautiful sea in the world was the one beside my house at San Salvador, but now I came to feel that the sea on which I looked from my new home was even more beautiful.

Once again I was able to take up a regular schedule of work. I resumed my daily routine—after my morning walk on the beach with Martita and after my communion with Bach at the piano—of practicing and composing. Indeed, before long I found myself busier than ever. Ideas that Governor Muñoz Marín and I had discussed only a year or so before were already taking shape. Aided by a special appropriation of the commonwealth legislature, and with the enthusiastic support of splendid Puerto Rican musicians, the first truly Puerto Rican symphony orchestra had been formed in San Juan. I did whatever I could to aid in its organization, and in the winter of 1958 I conducted its first public performance. The concert, at the thoughtful suggestion of Muñoz Marín, was held at my mother's birthplace, Mayagüez. Another development was the establishment of the Puerto Rico Conservatory of Music. I agreed to serve

A letter to Casals from Queen Elisabeth of Belgium, October 12, 1957. The letter reads: "Very dear Pau Casals, Thank you a thousand times for your most precious letter which has given me enormous pleasure. How happy I am, knowing dear little Martita, to learn that you are both united. My thoughts were very much with you when you were sick; what happiness that you have been able, with your splendid constitution and your well-known energy, to conquer the illness! I wish you the happiness you deserve, since you have given it with full hands—and your bow—to others, to humanity, which has so much need of goodness and beauty! Thank you for your touching thought in my grief for my sister, whom I miss so painfully. I hope I can see you again, dear Master, *dear* Pau Casals, next year in Prades if I can leave Brussels in 1957, when there will be much doing during the great world exposition. We shall be very busy here. Perhaps you will come with Martita to Stuyvenberg? I embrace you both with great affection. Your Elisabeth"

Stuyvenberg 12 oct. 1957

Très cher Pau Casals,

Merci mille fois pour votre si chère lettre qui m'a fait un énorme plaisir.

Comme je suis heureuse, connaissant la chère petite Martita, de vous savoir unis tous les deux.

Mes pensées ont été beaucoup avec vous pendant que vous étiez malade; quel bonheur que vous avez pu, avec votre belle constitution et votre énergie connue, vaincre le mal! Je vous souhaite le bonheur que vous méritez, puisque vous le donnez à pleines mains — et archet — aux autres, à l'humanité, qui a tant besoin de bonté et de beauté!

Merci de votre touchante pensée dans mon deuil pour ma sœur, qui me manque si douloureusement.

J'espère que je pourrai vous revoir, cher Maître, cher Pau Casals, l'année prochaine à Prades, si je peux partir de Bruxelles en 1957, où il y aura beaucoup de choses lors "la grande exposition universelle. Nous serons tous très pris ici. Peutêtre vous viendrez avec Martita au Stuyvenberg!

Je vous embrasse tous les deux avec grande affection,

Votre
Elisabeth

as its president, and we secured as its director the gifted Argentinian conductor and composer, Juan José Castro. This same Castro, remarkably enough, had been a violinist in the orchestra in which my brother Enrique played when he fled to Argentina some forty years before to avoid service in the Spanish army!

Martita participated in all of these undertakings with me, and, among other things, she became the cello teacher at the music conservatory. We had, of course, much other work to attend to. The second Festival Casals had taken place in San Juan that spring.

Though I was not yet ready to conduct—Schneider again led the orchestra—I played at a number of the concerts. And that same summer I returned to Prades to direct the three-week festival there. It was then that M. Barthelemey, the owner of the Grand Thermal Hotel, generously invited us to reside in a charming cottage adjoining this magnificent spa in the mountains about fifteen miles from Prades, and we were to occupy this cottage during future festivals.

Later that summer I received a letter from Estelle Caen, the head of the Music Extension of the University of California in Berkeley, inviting me to teach a series of master classes at the university. The idea appealed to me very much. I have always loved California—when I hear the word my heart stirs—and I knew of the splendid music department at the university. I agreed to come in the spring of 1960. Thirty-five years had then elapsed since my last visit to California and sixty years since my first. When Martita and I arrived in Berkeley my mind was full of memories. One of the most vivid was the day on Mount Tamalpais which had almost ended my musical career at the age of twenty-four. . . .

It was also in 1960 that I accepted an invitation from my

dear friend, Rudolf Serkin, to conduct master classes at the summer music festival he had been directing for several years at Marlboro, Vermont. Since then I have not missed a single summer at Marlboro. Over the years I have held classes in many parts of the world—in Paris, Berlin, Zermatt, Tokyo and other places—but the mood in Marlboro is unique. The surroundings themselves—the wooded hills and rolling farmland, the country lanes that wind among ponds and birch trees, the little towns with their old inns and churches—hold for me an ineffable charm and loveliness. I know of no place where I am more conscious of the affinity between nature and music. Marlboro is a veritable Arcady of music! And the approach to music too has a special quality. About a hundred musicians—well-known artists and young professionals—come to spend the summer months studying and playing, especially chamber music, for their own edification and pleasure. Their practice sessions take place in the simple white frame buildings—some of them are remodeled farmhouses—that form the campus of Marlboro College. The hall where my classes are held was once, I am told, a cow barn. There are informal concerts on weekdays and concerts attended by the public on weekends. . . . As you drive onto the campus, you pass a sign reading CAUTION—MUSICIANS AT PLAY. And all day the sound of musicians practicing pours from the windows of the buildings and mingles with the song of the birds! At Marlboro I find a special joy.

Yes, at my age I have much to be thankful for. I have my beloved Martita, my friends and the joy of my work. Yet I cannot say my heart is tranquil. How can one be at peace when there is such turmoil and anguish in the world? Who can rest when the very existence of mankind is imperiled?

I had hoped—like countless millions of others—that the

Дорогой и глубокоуважаемый маэстро
ПАБЛО КАЗАЛЬС!

Коллектив Московской государственной консерватории им. П. И. Чайковского шлет Вам сердечные поздравления к Вашему 84-летию.

В Вашем лице советские музыканты видят одного из наиболее прогрессивных художников и музыкальных деятелей нашего времени.

Вся Ваша долголетняя музыкально-исполнительская деятельность освещена высокими идеалами художественной правды и гуманизма. Вы всегда умели радовать сердца слушателей, облагораживать их.

Мы знаем о тех дружеских и творческих отношениях, которые связали Вас с такими видными русскими музыкантами, как Н. А. Римский-Корсаков, А. К. Глазунов, А. Н. Скрябин, С. В. Рахманинов, А. Б. Гольденвейзер.

Старшее поколение советских музыкантов тепло вспоминает Ваши концерты в Москве и в других городах нашей страны. Ваши грамзаписи знают и изучают молодые советские музыканты.

Мы глубоко ценим исключительную художественность Вашей интерпретации, ее подлинно-творческий характер, Ваше высокое мастерство.

Вас, дорогой маэстро, глубоко уважают в нашей стране не только как выдающегося музыканта, но и как передового человека нашего времени, горячо любящего свою родину и свой народ, как убежденного антифашиста и борца за мир и дружбу народов во всем мире.

Искренне желаем Вам, дорогой друг, многих лет жизни, здоровья и больших творческих успехов.

victory over fascism in the Second World War would bring great changes to the world. I had looked to a time of new freedom and amity among the nations. Instead, the cold war came with its atom bomb tests, rearmament and bitter strife. When I visited the United States a decade and a half after the defeat of the Axis—after a war in which some fifty million human beings had perished—people were building private air-raid shelters. I read with horror about atom bomb drills in the schools—drills in which children were taught to crouch in corners and hide under desks. To me all this was madness—I knew that the only defense against atom bombs was peace.

In the summer of 1958 I joined Albert Schweitzer in an appeal to the American and Russian governments to end the arms race and ban all future nuclear tests. In a public

←————————————————————

A message to Casals signed by forty members of the Moscow State Conservatory on the occasion of his 84th birthday in 1960. The message reads: "Dear and deeply respected Maestro Pablo Casals: The organization of the Moscow State Conservatory, known as the P. I. Tchaikovsky Conservatory, sends your heartfelt congratulations on your 84th anniversary. In your face, Soviet musicians see one of the most progressive artists and concerned musicians of our time. All of your many years of musical activity are illuminated by ideas of artistic truth and humanism. You have always known how to gladden the hearts of listeners and to ennoble them. We know of the warm and creative ties you had with such great Russian musicians as N. A. Rimski-Korsakov, A. K. Glazunov, A. N. Scriabin, S. V. Rachmaninoff, and A. B. Goldenvayzen. The oldest generation of Soviet musicians warmly remembers your concerts in Moscow and other cities in our country. Your recordings are known and studied by young musicians. We deeply value the unique artistry of your interpretations, which bear your own creative character and great mastery. You, dear Maestro, are deeply respected in our country not only as an outstanding musician but as one of the advanced men of our times. You are warmly loved by the people of our motherland as a dedicated anti-fascist and fighter for peace and friendship among the people of the whole world. With all our heart we wish you, dear friend, many years of life, health and great creative accomplishment."

statement I said, "I hope that the United States and Russia will overlook their political differences in the long-range interests of mankind. It is incredible that civilized men can continue to build new and more destructive weapons instead of devoting their energies toward making this a happier and more beautiful world."

Soon afterwards I was invited to play before the United Nations at a ceremony commemorating the thirteenth anniversary of its formation. In my eyes this international forum—despite all the problems and obstacles that beset it—represented the greatest hope for building peace among the nations, and I gratefully welcomed the opportunity to use my music in that cause. The concert on that occasion was a most extraordinary event. It was transmitted by television and radio to seventy-four nations throughout the world. Never before had a message of music reached an audience of so many million human beings. Together with Horszowski, I played at the great General Assembly Hall of the UN headquarters in New York City—we played Bach's Sonata No. 2 in D Major for cello and piano. The program then continued from Paris with performances by the American violinist, Yehudi Menuhin; the Russian violinist, David Oistrakh; and the Indian sitar player, Ravi Shankar. The concert concluded with the Orchestre de la Suisse Romande in Geneva performing the last movement of Beethoven's Ninth Symphony with a chorus and soloists from Great Britain.

I had written a message for the occasion, which was distributed among the audience at the General Assembly Hall before I played. "If at my age I come here for this day," I stated, "it is not because anything has changed in my moral attitude or in the restrictions I have imposed upon myself and my career as an artist for all these years, but because all else becomes secondary in comparison to the great and perhaps mortal danger threatening all humanity."

LEOPOLD STOKOWSKI

16 Nov 61

Dear Master and Friend

    I shall always remember and treasure hearing
you play again, so superbly, with such beauty of tone
and phrasing, and such deep expression. Thank you
for this unforgetable experience. How wonderful is
that music of Couperin. I am hoping to go to Puerto
Rico at Christmas time. May I have the pleasure of
visiting you and your beautiful bride? I shall bring
my two sons, and, of course, we shall not take too
much of your time.

                    Sincerely, your admirer and friend

1067 Fifth Avenue
New York 28, New York

AT 9-3689

A letter to Casals from Leopold Stokowski, November 16, 1961

I went on to say:

*The anguish of the world caused by the continuation of
nuclear danger is increasing every day. . . . How I wish that
there could be a tremendous movement of protest in all
countries, and especially from the mothers, that would im-
press those who have the power to prevent this catastrophe!*

*Those who believe in the dignity of man should act at
this time to bring about a deeper understanding among
people and a sincere rapprochement between conflicting
forces. The United Nations today represents the most important hope for peace. Let us give it all power to act for*

*our benefit. And let us fervently pray that the near future
will disperse the clouds that darken our days now.*

In the immediately ensuing years I used every meaningful opportunity to raise my voice in the cause of peace, and
I joined the boards of several organizations—like the Committee for a Sane Nuclear Policy—which were working to
arouse people to the menace of atomic warfare. But I was
not satisfied with these efforts of mine. I felt the need to
act with deeds, not words. All my life, music had been my
only weapon. How then, I asked myself, could I best use
this weapon now? A plan took form in my mind. It revolved
around my oratorio *El Pessebre*, "The Manger," for which
I had composed the music in Prades during the war. Since
the message of this work was peace and the brotherhood
of man, what better vehicle had I for acting at this urgent
hour? I decided to take the oratorio anywhere in the world
that I could and conduct it as a personal message in the
cause of international understanding and world peace.

Some of my friends sought to dissuade me from the undertaking—they were concerned that it might prove too
arduous for me. It was of course true, as they pointed out,
that I was approaching my eighty-fifth birthday. But it
seemed to me that the very fact I might not have much
longer on this earth was all the more reason for acting
while I could. Early in 1962 I announced my intention of
embarking on a personal peace crusade with *El Pessebre*.

"I am a man first, an artist second," I stated. "As a man,
my first obligation is to the welfare of my fellow men. I
will endeavor to meet this obligation through music—the
means which God has given me—since it transcends language, politics and national boundaries. My contribution to
world peace may be small. But at least I will have given all
I can to an ideal I hold sacred."

Whatever financial benefits came from the performances of my oratorio, I said, would go to a fund I was establishing to promote causes dedicated to human dignity, fraternity and peace. . . .

The first performance of *El Pessebre* in my peace crusade took place that spring in the city of San Francisco. It was held in the Memorial Opera House, where the founding articles of the United Nations had been signed at the end of the war. The auditorium was filled to overflowing—hundreds were standing—and the audience's response to the music meant to me that they understood its message and fervently shared my longing for a peaceful world.

The response has been the same wherever I have taken *El Pessebre*—and I have given performances in North and South America, in England and France, in Italy, Germany, Hungary, Israel and a dozen other lands. Everywhere, people have demonstrated the same hunger for peace, the same desire to join their fellow men in building a world pledged to human happiness. Every performance has been for me a reaffirmation of my conviction that it is not the peoples of the world but artificial barriers imposed by their governments that hold them apart.

Two performances of *El Pessebre* stand out especially in my mind. They occurred under greatly contrasting circumstances, and yet there was a particular affinity between them. One was held at the United Nations headquarters in New York City; the other in the ruins of the Abbey of Saint-Michel de Cuxa in southern France.

The performance at Saint-Michel de Cuxa—which took place in the fall of 1966 as I approached my ninetieth birthday—commemorated the nine-hundredth anniversary of the Catalan Assembly of Tologes. That Assembly was an event of historic import. From it evolved the earliest parliament and first representative form of government in continental Europe. The proclamation of the Assembly—*Pau i Treva de Deu* or "Peace and Truce of the Lord"—called for the end of war as a means of settling disputes between nations and for peace among all peoples. And to think this proclamation was made almost a thousand years before the founding of the United Nations! One can imagine my emotions when I conducted *El Pessebre* in that ancient shrine on that occasion. . . .

The performance at the United Nations occurred toward the end of October in 1963. Five years had elapsed since my previous appearance at the UN and almost two decades since the end of the Second World War—yet peace still seemed far distant. The missile crisis in Cuba—when the whole world had been on the brink of nuclear disaster—was fresh in everybody's mind; and there were already ominous rumblings of impending civil war in Vietnam. Who could say what perils lay ahead? My spirit was heavy with apprehensions, and yet the very nature of the occasion gave cause for hope. . . .

I confided my feelings to U Thant, the Secretary General of the UN, when he graciously invited me to rest in his private office after a rehearsal of my oratorio. While we were talking, I noticed on a table a display of miniature flags of all the countries forming the United Nations. "What a wonderful thing!" I told U Thant. "To have before you every day this symbol of the time when the nations of the world will stand side by side, free and equal and at peace!" A few days after my return to Puerto Rico, a package arrived at my house. It contained the flags of the United Nations! That good and dedicated man had sent them to me as a gift. Today they hang on the wall of the living room of my home in Santurce. . . .

At the UN concert, I delivered a message which concluded with these words: "Music, that wonderful universal language, should be a source of communication among men. I once again exhort my fellow musicians throughout the world to put the purity of their art at the service of mankind in order to unite all people in fraternal ties. Let each of us contribute as he is able until this ideal is attained in all its glory."

One month later the hopes of peace suffered an appalling blow that brought grief to all the nations of the world. It was then that President Kennedy was assassinated.

I had first met President Kennedy in the fall of 1961 when he invited me to play at a concert at the White House. For some time I had deeply admired the President. For me he exemplified qualities of idealism and leadership which were desperately needed in the crisis facing the world, and after his election I wrote him saying I rejoiced in his victory as a propitious omen for all humanity. I indicated my fervent hope that the principles of freedom and human dignity he espoused would hasten the return of democracy in my own beloved land. President Kennedy replied with a letter graciously thanking me for my expression of confidence in him.

However, despite my respect and admiration for the President, I hesitated before accepting the invitation to play at the White House. I wanted to be sure that my appearance would not seem to imply I had modified in any way my abhorrence of the Franco dictatorship in Spain or my opinion of the immorality of supporting this regime. But I decided that the overriding consideration was that my visit to the White House might advance my efforts in behalf of peace and enable me to raise again with the President the question of freedom in Spain. "I know that your aim," I wrote to President Kennedy in a letter accepting his invitation, "is to work for peace based on justice, understanding and freedom for all mankind. These ideals have always been my ideals, and have determined the most important decisions—and the most important renunciations—in my life."

The concert took place on the evening of November 13— almost sixty years after my first appearance at the White House. It was one of the most meaningful events of my life. After a dinner honoring Governor Muñoz Marín of Puerto Rico, about one hundred and fifty guests of the President gathered in the East Room of the White House. There my friends Mieczyslaw Horszowski and Alexander Schneider joined me in a program of chamber music by Mendelssohn, Schumann and Couperin. At the end of the program I interrupted the applause. "Now," I said, "I want to play a Catalan folk song." And I played "The Song of the Birds," the theme of the Spanish exiles, to convey what was closest to my heart—freedom for my people. Then I walked to where the President was seated, and we embraced.

Earlier that day, at President Kennedy's invitation, I had met privately with him at the White House. He took me to a small room, where we sat together alone and talked. I felt immensely drawn to him—he was so natural and unpretentious, so young and yet so wise and human. "It is a strange thing," I told him, "but I feel that I have known you always." And he said yes, that he too shared this feeling.

Ordinarily, on such occasions, a secretary comes and goes. You feel the pressure of time. But in this case there was nothing like that. After a while I said, "Mr. President, I think I am taking too much of your time." He replied, "Please do not feel this way. It is a privilege for me. Please let us keep talking." I said, "Thank you, bless you."

We spoke about many things, about his experiences and my childhood, about the grievous conditions in the world. I brought up the matter of Spain. I told the President how much I deplored the fact that American military bases had been established in Spain and that Franco was receiving aid from the democratic powers. He listened gravely—his expression reflected his sympathy. A President, he told me, invariably inherited certain problems and could not always act as he himself might most desire to. He intended, he said, to do everything in his power toward securing peace and liberty everywhere in the world. In my heart I felt that this man would do all he could for my people. Finally I said, "Mr. President, I cannot take any more of your time." And I insisted on leaving.

In the evening, after the concert, the President and Mrs. Kennedy arranged a small private supper—my colleagues and I had not eaten before the performance. Toward the end of the meal one of the President's aides brought him a message. "I am terribly sorry," President Kennedy told me, "but there is a matter I have to attend to." And he left.

It was very cold that evening, but Jacqueline Kennedy insisted on accompanying Martita and me to our car. She was without a coat—she was wearing an evening dress— and I was afraid she might catch cold. I asked her please not to come outside. But she said, "The President would want me to—and I myself want to." She stood there, in the cold, waiting as we drove away.

The following morning a magnificent bouquet of flowers from the President and Jacqueline Kennedy arrived at the hotel where Martita and I were staying. They were accompanied by a letter from the President in which he expressed with great warmth his appreciation for the evening we had spent together.

On my return home, I wrote the President, "Last Monday night I played with all my heart—and I feel that the results have been rewarding. I am grateful if my humble tribute to you may have at the same time contributed to

THE WHITE HOUSE

WASHINGTON

November 14, 1961

Dear Maestro Casals,

Mrs. Kennedy and I can never express our full appreciation for what you did last night. You gave honor to our country, to The White House, and to the world of music. There are very few unforgettable evenings, but everyone who was present last night will regard this one as such.

The enthralled audience who listened to every beautiful note of the concert was testimony enough to your success. However, Mrs. Kennedy and I will always be grateful that you came to play for us. It was an evening that made us feel humble and it was an evening that gave inspiration and encouragement to lovers of music throughout this country.

My wife joins me in sending all best wishes to you and to Madame Casals,

Sincerely,

Mr. Pablo Casals
Hay Adams
800 16th Street, N. W.
Washington, D. C.

A letter from President Kennedy to Casals following his performance at the White House in 1961

SIXTEENTH AT H STREET, N.W.
WASHINGTON 6. D. C.

Nov. 14ᵗʰ 1961

copy

Mr President

To have met you and mrs. Kennedy has been
a privilege which will be unforgettable for me and
mrs Casals

I am deeply honored and grateful for your
kindness and generous attentions.

May I repeat to you my respects and my
conviction that the whole world looks upon you with
hope and confidence.

May God inspire you, Mr President and
bless you and your family —

I have been moved by your delicate thought
in sending the flowers which have given me much
pleasure to me and my wife.

Please accept, Mr President, together with mrs.
Kennedy our deepest appreciation and, if — I may
say our affectionate thoughts
— P. C.

Casals' draft of a letter to President Kennedy after the White House
performance

music and culture. The whole of November 13th will always have a special meaning for me. My visit and conversation with you have strengthened and confirmed my faith and hopes for our ideals of Peace and Freedom. Thank you, Mr. President."

I was to see President Kennedy on only one other occasion. That was when he visited Puerto Rico in the summer of 1963 as a guest of Governor Muñoz Marín. I attended the dinner at La Fortaleza in the President's honor. In his speech he paid me a tribute that touched me deeply. That fall I received a message from him informing me he wished to confer on me the Presidential Medal of Freedom. He invited me to Washington to receive the award. Shortly before the designated date, there came that awful day of his death.

Because Martita knew what this great and dear man meant to me, she kept the news from me at first. All that afternoon friends came to see me at my house, but Martita told them not to tell me what had happened. I learned the news that evening. I have seen much of suffering and death in my lifetime, but I have never lived through a more terrible moment. For hours I could not speak. It was as if a beautiful and irreplaceable part of the world had suddenly been torn away. What a tragic horror that this young father and gallant leader on whom the hopes of mankind centered should be struck down in the street by an assassin's bullet! What monstrous madness!

Who knows what might have happened had President Kennedy lived? No single man, of course, controls the fate of all nations, and yet during his brief time as President one felt how his hand moved to heal the wounds and conflicts of the world. What savage strife we have witnessed since his death! Had he not died, how many of those who have perished in the towns and jungles of Vietnam might also be alive?

Sometimes I look about me with a feeling of complete dismay. In the confusion that afflicts the world today, I see a disrespect for the very values of life. Beauty is all about us, but how many are blind to it! They look at the wonder of this earth—and seem to see nothing. People move hectically but give little thought to where they are going. They seek excitement for its mere sake, as if they were lost and desperate. They take little pleasure in the natural and quiet and simple things of life.

Each second we live in a new and unique moment of the universe, a moment that never was before and will never be again. And what do we teach our children in school? We teach them that two and two make four, and that Paris is the capital of France. When will we also teach them what they are? We should say to each of them: Do you know what you are? You are a marvel. You are unique. In all of the world there is no other child exactly like you. In the millions of years that have passed there has never been another child like you. And look at your body—what a wonder it is! your legs, your arms, your cunning fingers, the way you move! You may become a Shakespeare, a Michelangelo, a Beethoven. You have the capacity for anything. Yes, you are a marvel. And when you grow up, can you then harm another who is, like you, a marvel? You must cherish one another. You must work—we all must work— to make this world worthy of its children.

What extraordinary changes and advances I have witnessed in my lifetime! What amazing progress—in science, industry, the exploration of space! And yet hunger, racial oppression and tyranny still torment the world. We continue to act like barbarians. Like savages, we fear our neighbors on this earth—we arm against them, and they arm against us. I deplore to have had to live at a time when man's law is to kill. When shall we become accustomed to the fact that we are human beings?

The Annual Hiroshima Day Peace Citation which was awarded Casals in 1962

The love of one's country is a natural thing. But why should love stop at the border? Our family is one—each of us has a duty to his brothers. We are all leaves of a tree, and the tree is humanity.

Not long ago Martita and I had a little country house built near the village of Ceiba on the coast about fifty miles from San Juan. We have christened the house *El Pessebre.* It is high on a hillside among fields of sugar cane. Beneath us stretches a great span of ocean with a shoreline fringed by palm trees and with green islands rising from the sea. The skies there are incredible—I have never seen such sunsets and such fantastic cloud formations! The wind comes in all day from the ocean—we are, I am told, in the direct path of trade winds that blow across the Atlantic the year round, the same winds that brought Columbus here from Spain five hundred years ago. Occasionally the wind gets very strong—the roof of our house is anchored to the ground by cables, and they sometimes hum at night like strange musical instruments.

Now when we are in Puerto Rico, we spend our weekends whenever possible at *El Pessebre.* How I love that place! It reminds me of San Salvador. Our dear friends, Rosa and Luis Cueto Coll, often accompany us, and in the evenings the four of us play dominoes together. Rosa is my partner—she plays a splendid game. We keep a running score, and Rosa and I are usually a good many points ahead of Martita and Luis. "Don't get discouraged," I tell them. "You may catch up with us when I'm one hundred."

Martita and I met the Cueto Colls soon after we came to Puerto Rico, and they have since become our intimate friends. They often accompany us to music festivals or when I'm traveling with *El Pessebre.* When we first became friends, I did not know that two of Luis' uncles had fought with the Loyalist army in Spain—one, Juan Cueto, was a lieutenant colonel in command of the Basque front—and both of them were captured by the Fascists and shot. Luis' father Augusto Cueto, was a merchant in Puerto Rico who lost his business during the Spanish Civil War because he devoted all his time to an organization he'd founded to help the Republican cause—this man's last thoughts were of Spain, and when he died after the fall of the Republic his final gesture was to raise his fist in the Loyalist salute.

I keep in close touch with the situation in Spain. Each week I receive from Barcelona a package full of clippings from different newspapers and magazines. They concern all news of possible interest—political, cultural, economic, sports. They are sent to me by a Catalan friend—a man I met only when he came to Prades. He is a man of modest means, but he has made it his task to send me these clippings every week without fail.

I continue to serve as the honorary chairman of Spanish Refugee Aid—the organization was founded in New York following the Second World War to help those Spanish anti-fascist refugees who were destitute in France. Though large numbers of my exiled compatriots have taken up jobs in France or settled in Latin America, there are still thousands in France who are sick and old and poverty-stricken; many of them were crippled in the Civil War or, later, fighting with the Allied forces against Hitler. The conditions under which they exist are heart-rending. They live in slums or rural shacks, mostly in southern France; and they have the barest necessities—many survive on incomes of less

---

Casals' message to the *Pacem in Terris* Convocation in Geneva, at which his peace oratorio, *El Pessebre*, was performed on May 29, 1967

I speak to you from my home in Puerto Rico, but my heart is with you at your gathering in Geneva. I had hoped to be present at your urgently important convocation and to have the privilege of conducting in your company my oratorio *El Pessebre*, which is dedicated to the cause of peace. But, I have just recovered from an operation, and my doctors tell me I cannot fulfill my desire to come to Geneva.

The purpose of your meeting is that which has long been dearest to me — the purpose of peace, peace for all men in all parts of the world. When I see innocent blood spilled and the tears of the victims of injustice, it becomes more important to me than all my music.

We live in an age in which men have accomplished magnificent things and made miraculous advances, an age in which man embarks upon the exploration of the stars. Yet, on our own planet we continue to act as barbarians. Like barbarians we fear our neighbors on this earth; we arm against them and they arm against us. The time has come when this must be halted if man is to survive. We must become accustomed to the fact we are human beings.

The love of one's country is a splendid thing. But why should love stop at the border? There is a brotherhood among all men. This must be recognized if life is to remain. We must learn the love of man.

It is profoundly meaningful to me that your convocation, *Pacem in Terris*, "Peace on Earth," derives from that noble encyclical of Pope John XXIII, in which with such eloquence and enlightenment he called for peace and coexistence between the different ideologies and nations of the world. How else, indeed, can peace come to our tortured earth? And lacking peace, what in this nuclear age will be left of that earth?

In the words of Pope John, "It is hardly possible to imagine that in the atomic era, war could be used as an instrument of justice." And yet today war is being waged.

As I sit by these peaceful shores of the Caribbean Sea, the killing continues in Vietnam. This must stop; this terrible war must be ended! From one end of the world to the other, the cry must resound: we have had enough of death! We demand the right of life!

Dear friends, my only weapons for justice and against war have been my cello and my conductor's baton; and though I cannot be with you, my music will speak for me of love and peace. And not only my music but another part of me. For it is my dear brother, Enric, who conducts my *El Pessebre*, and the voices you hear are those of soloists and chorus who have worked long and intimately with me.

May God bless you, dear friends! May your deliberations hasten the end of war and the beginning of a joyous future for all mankind!

Pablo Casals

than fifty cents a day. To send them food and clothing and medical supplies, or money for coal and wood or for scholarships for their children—that is not charity, for these men and women are owed a debt that, alas, can never be repaid.

Many people have forgotten what happened in Spain. They do not think about the refugees who sacrificed everything in freedom's cause. But justice and morality demand that these things be remembered—and, above all, the fact that the Spanish people still live under the yoke of tyranny. Recently, after Richard Nixon was elected President of the United States, I wrote him a letter about the situation in Spain. Once again I stated my longing to see democracy restored in my long-suffering country and my abhorrence of the dictatorship that had been established there with Hitler's and Mussolini's aid. "I am hoping," I wrote President Nixon, "that your country—so noted for its struggle for freedom—will reappraise its attitude toward the Franco regime in order to decide whether or not it should continue to help the harsh Spanish dictatorship, as it has been doing during the last thirty years." I received a noncommittal reply from one of the President's assistants.

Of course there have been important developments in recent years. The struggle against the dictatorship has grown throughout Spain—among students, workers, intellectuals, members of the clergy—and they have forced the regime to make certain concessions. And there are even articles about me now in the Spanish press—for years after Franco came to power it was not permitted to mention my name. Of course the articles today speak only about my music, never about my political opinions. When friends of mine recently visited the Spanish Travel Bureau in New York City, they were given promotional literature which referred to me as one of the prominent citizens of Spain— it neglected, however, to state I live in exile!

Not long ago a friend of mine who was visiting Puerto Rico mentioned he was feeling homesick—he had, he said, been away from his home for more than three weeks. "I understand what you mean," I told him. "I have been away from home for more than thirty years."

Perhaps I shall never see Catalonia again. For years I believed that freedom would come again to my beloved land before I died. Now I am unsure. It will come, I know, and I rejoice in that knowledge. But for me it is a sadness that I may not live to see it.

I have, after all, lived quite a long time, and I do not expect to live forever. I do not look toward death with fear. It is a natural thing, as natural as being born. But I do have regrets. I regret to leave the world in such a sorry state. I regret that Martita, my family and my friends will feel sorrow.

Of course I continue to play and to practice. I think I would do so if I lived for another hundred years. I could not betray my old friend, the cello.

ACKNOWLEDGMENTS

During the initial phase of my work on this book, I consulted various published works on Casals which provided me with valuable background material for our subsequent discussions regarding his early years. Among the most useful of these works were Joan Alavedra's *Pablo Casals*, J. Ma. Corredor's *Conversations with Casals*, Lillian Littlehale's *Pablo Casals*, and Bernard Taper's *Cellist In Exile*. In connection with my general research, I made frequent reference to the rich materials available at the music library of the University of California, Berkeley, and I am indebted to its head, Professor Vincent Duckles, for his generous assistance. Other valuable reference sources were the fine music collection at the Sonoma County Public Library in Santa Rosa, California; and, especially for current data, the files at the New York office of Festival Casals, whose music secretary, Dinorah Press, was greatly helpful.

I am indebted to Rosa and Luis Cueto Coll for more favors than I can recount and for the heartwarming hospitality they extended to me whenever I visited Puerto Rico. I am also grateful to Doris Madden for her friendly suggestions and enthusiastic support; and to Professor Alfredo Matilla of the University of Puerto Rico for his considerate aid.

My thanks must go to Josefina de Frondizi, not only for her painstaking examination of various Spanish materials but also for her warm interest in the whole undertaking; to my son, Timothy, for his valuable assistance in various aspects of my research and especially in my survey of Casals' papers and memorabilia at Molitg-les-Bains, France, and San Salvador, Spain; and to Luis and Enrique Casals for their gracious help when I visited Spain. I am also grateful for thoughtful aid from Alexander Schneider, Rudolf Serkin and Mieczyslaw Horszowski.

I must record a special indebtedness to Peter Schwed of Simon and Schuster, whose wise counsel and constant encouragement were indispensable to my work. I am grateful to my editor, Charlotte Seitlin, for her solicitous attention to this undertaking in all its phases; to Edith Fowler for sensitive understanding in the book's design; and to Ann Maulsby for exacting care in styling the manuscript.

I wish to express my deep appreciation to Louis Honig for his unflagging interest and perceptive editorial comment, and for presenting a group of my Casals photographs to the Stanford University Library. On more than one occasion Richard O. Boyer gave me advice and support, for which I owe him much. I am obligated to A. Cameron for reading the opening portion of the manuscript. My thanks are due Professor Fred Warren, Daniel Koshland, Estelle Caen, Edwin Berry Burgum, Robert Kahan, David Grutman, Betty and Samuel Katzin, Harry Margolis, Jack Froom and Sara Gordon for facilitating various aspects of this work.

I am indebted to the Samuel Rubin Foundation for making possible a permanent museum collection of my photographs of Casals, and to Cyma Rubin for her enthusiastic and creative interest in this work.

To Riette, my wife, I owe special gratitude for her patient, unremitting and invaluable assistance in all phases of this work.

There are no words with which to express my indebtedness to Marta and Pablo Casals for their patient help, hospitality and friendship, without which this book could never have taken form.

A.E.K.

INDEX

[Page numbers in italics denote illustrations]

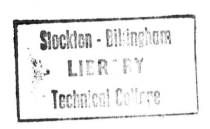

ABOUT ALBERT E. KAHN

A writer of singular versatility, Mr. Kahn is widely known as the author of political exposés. His book *Sabotage!*, dealing with Axis conspiratorial activities, was one of the top best sellers of the Second World War, and his subsequent books on secret diplomacy and fascist intrigue have been translated into more than twenty languages. His book *Days with Ulanova* was hailed as a work of major importance on the ballet. Mr. Kahn's photographs of the famous Russian ballerina form a permanent collection at the Library and Museum of the Performing Arts of the New York Public Library at Lincoln Center. His most recent books have been *Smetana and the Beetles* and *The Unholy Hymnal*, for which he won attention as an incisive satirist.

Born in London, England, Mr. Kahn is a graduate of Dartmouth College, where he was an outstanding athlete and winner of the Crawford Campbell Literary Fellowship. He is married, has three sons, and now lives in Glen Ellen, California.